THE

RULES

*THE T MEANS THE TRUTH

RULE no. 14
Keep it real,
EXCEPT FOR YOUR TITS.
p.119

RULE no. 15
If there's a crowd, work it.
p.126

RULE no. 16
Friend up.
p.144

RULE no. 17
SCREW THE PENIS CLUB
(Figuratively speaking, darling.)
p.150

RULE no. 18
Never trust a man in Dockers.
p.159

RULE no. 19
Project positivity,
EVEN WHEN YOU FEEL LIKE SHIT.
p.166

RULE no. 20
Act like a Star,
EVEN IF NO ONE'S WATCHING.
p.171

RULE no. 21
If you take no for an answer twice,
YOU'RE F*CKING UP.
p.182

RULE no. 22
Stop relying on that body.
p.188

RULE no. 23
Make magic.
p.195

RULE no. 24
Make your boss look good.
p.197

RULE no. 25
Build your legacy.
p.203

ACKNOWLEDGMENTS: p.210

MICHELLE VISAGE

is a

highly intelligent, fiercely loyal, and hyper-aware. Like a skilled hunter, she is always in search of the next conquest. And without fail, she has the amazing ability to always land on her feet.

I first laid eyes on this beautiful creature in 1988 at "The Love Ball," an annual charity event that brought all the "Vogueing Houses" of New York City together for a good cause. That was her chosen scene at the time, amongst the streetwise black and Latino gay kids of the urban jungle. The same gay kids that were forever immortalized in Jenny Livingston's documentary *Paris Is Burning*.

Michelle stood out, not only because she was a straight white Jewish girl from South Plainfield, New Jersey, but because she had "it," that undeniable star quality.

I later learned that the "ballroom" scene was just the latest of several scenes that Michelle had already explored and had perfectly morphed herself into. Being an expert shape-shifter would eventually become her calling card.

The next time I saw Michelle, she was being escorted across the dance floor at club Red Zone in Midtown. Initially, I didn't recognize her with newly-bleached platinum blonde hair and a skintight gown that allowed her to only take tiny, deliberate steps, giving everyone watching enough time to soak in all the glamour. I remember asking "who's that girl?" and a friend telling me that she was a member of Seduction, the girl-group performing that night.

Watching Michelle tiptoe across that dance floor became one of those mental GIFS that my mind collected for no apparent reason at the time, but would later prove to be a valuable piece of a much bigger puzzle.

Within a year, Michelle's face was everywhere. Seduction had become a huge hit with a chart-topping album and music videos in heavy rotation. Unfortunately, the group disbanded after a year, but Michelle Visage is unstoppable. She re-emerged in yet another chart-topping group called S.O.U.L. System.

It was during this period that I realized just how ambitious this young woman was, and that she also had the work ethic to back it up.

In 1992, Michelle and I were reintroduced at a promotional concert hosted by a New York radio station. Her group was one of several acts performing at the event, and so was I. We had a fabulous time laughing and carrying on backstage. That's when I realized how smart, funny and irreverent she was. That meeting was yet another clue that this girl was someone who would eventually play a huge part in my life.

Fast forward to 1996. I walked into a radio interview, and much to my surprise, there she was, sitting behind the microphone cohosting a morning-drive radio show.

Same charming, hilarious Michelle, but she had become a redhead and completely morphed herself into an on-air radio personality. *Le caméléon brillante.*

In hindsight, I shouldn't have been surprised. I'd seen enough of her incarnations to know that she was anything but predictable. I was so happy to see her because I knew that what would've been the same old typical "morning zoo" radio interview would now be a continuation of the laugh riot we'd had years prior.

The station's program director heard our natural chemistry on-air and said, "I found my new morning crew." From that moment on, Michelle and I have been partners. With lightning speed, our broadcast became a top three morning-drive radio show in the New York tri-state area. That's when I asked Michelle to join me on VH1's TV talker *The RuPaul Show*.

Being charismatic, articulate, and absolutely gorgeous enabled Michelle to navigate easily between the two mediums. She's also naturally inquisitive and eerily perceptive. Nothing at all slips by this woman.

When *RuPaul's Drag Race* was conceived, there was no question that Michelle Visage would have a seat on the judge's panel. Unfortunately, at the time, she was under contract to a Florida radio station that wouldn't allow her to take a leave of absence and come to Hollywood for filming.

So, the first two seasons of the TV show were filmed without Michelle as a judge, and her presence was truly missed. I really needed her unique voice on that panel to bounce off of. Truth be told, she makes my job so much easier and enjoyable. I missed my friend.

Plus, she knows the world of drag (she's a drag queen herself), she speaks the same language as our street savvy contestants, and she knows the art of creating a persona that reflects what the environment calls for. On top of all that, she's a compassionate defender of the disenfranchised. After two long years, I got my wish.

Finally, Michelle took her rightful place on the judges' panel for the third season. Right where she belongs. And for all the obvious reasons, our show was elevated to the next level of beauty, heart, and soul. Because that's what Michelle Visage is.

The contestants respect her opinion, and they trust her because she has walked the walk. I've always jokingly said that Michelle is a gay man trapped in a woman's body, but for more that just her love of the outrageous. Her X-ray eyes can see through to the core, and dissect any issue the way only an outsider can. She's the first to recognize when "the Emperor has no clothes on."

And that's what makes her such a fascinating, and intriguing woman. There are lessons to be learned, my children. And Michelle Visage is here to teach them.

She's my friend, my business partner and she is someone I admire very much. I love this woman, and in reading this book, I know that you will fall in love with her too.

—RUPAUL

INTRODUCTION

Doll, if you don't know me from my early days Vogueing at parties at New York's famed Copacabana Club with the legendary party promoter Susanne Bartsch, or topping the pop charts with my girl group Seduction in the nineties, or co-hosting a talk show on VH1 with my 6'4" BFF RuPaul, or deejaying the morning drives on hit radio stations in New York City, Los Angeles, West Palm Beach, or Miami, then, at least you probably know me from my most recent gigs: a player in the Hell House known as *Celebrity Big Brother UK* and/or more importantly as judge on *RuPaul's Drag Race.* And if you do know me from *Drag Race,* then maybe, like many of the queens on the show, you might even fear me a little bit, but don't be scared. Please. I may be a proud no-nonsense bitch who will always call you on your bullshit when I see it, but it comes from a place of love, respect, and admiration. I'm *all* about being real—except for the tits—and I'm here for one thing and one thing only: To help you achieve your dreams.

So, all of you ridiculously beautiful girls and gays out there, consider yourselves my divas-in-training, because here's the thing: You *already* have what it takes to be the star of your own life. You already are fabulous. I can't give that to you. I can't make you have that "it" factor; that thing that makes you genuine, generous, and grand; that magnetism that makes people want to be near you, just because they feel better about themselves and the world when they're around you. It's in you. You were born a diva. We all were. Think about it: As babies, none of us were afraid to demand attention, make noise, cry out for love, be in our bodies, laugh, sing, play, dance, experiment. We ruled every room, and it felt perfectly natural, because we never once even thought to question our right to be completely amazing, to take up space, to be purely ourselves. And then, we grow up and screw up. We get self-consciousness. We allow insecurities to sneak in. We start to harbor shame for who we are (or who we want to be). And before long, that twinkle in our eyes starts to fade. Our God-given glitter—gasp!—comes unglued. And we start making decisions based not on what's spectacular, but on what's safe. Most people live that way, and there's absolutely nothing wrong with that—for them. But not for you. You owe it to yourself to nurture the inner diva that lives within and I am going to show you how to do that and more.

Remember this: the journey is not always going to be easy, but it will be worth it. Maybe you are lucky, and you love what you do and rock it every day. But, unless your name is Mariah, being a diva doesn't always pay the bills. And until it does, you need a day job. There's no shame in that. We all do whatever it takes to survive. But always, always remember this: Just because you have to clock in from nine to five, or work on the assembly line, or field customer service calls all day, or shuffle papers, or sell shit you don't give a shit about doesn't mean you have to ever stop being fabulous. Wherever you work, whatever you do, you can be a diva, and being your fabulous self will help you get where you want to go.

Take it from me: I've used the skills I acquired working it in the Harlem ball scene, in the dance clubs (and, yes, strip clubs), on the radio, on the road, and now on TV to build an amazing life for myself (and, as the sole breadwinner for my family, also for my husband, who stays home to help raise our two daughters. I'm a lucky lady). Being a diva is not just what I do, it's also who I am. And it's the reason why I've been so successful in my life. And no matter what area of your life you want to lead in—whether in fashion, music, drag, love, or library sciences, it doesn't matter—my rules will help you get to the top.

So, listen up, children, and I'll tell you how I became the diva I am today. I'll share with you the juicy stories behind my biggest life lessons, and then I'll teach you exactly how to work it harder, better, and smarter than anyone else. Use my own personal rules for success to guide you in work and life, and I guarantee, you'll earn that promotion, land that role, get that guy, whatever you want. But most important, when you look at yourself in the mirror every morning, you'll love the strong, sexy, powerful doll looking back at you. Soon enough, you'll rule every room and, before long, the entire world.

RULE _no._ 1:

LIVE BY THE THREE TENETS OF DIVAHOOD.

If, when you hear the word "diva," you're picturing some starlet sitting on a chaise, being fanned by a tanned Greek god in a loincloth, well, hell, just close your eyes and keep picturing that for a little while. Loincloths are hot. Once you feel like you've had your fill of fantasy, let this secret sink into your beautiful little noggin: There's a better way to be a diva. So right here, right now, before we go any further, I'm going to give you the T. (That's the Truth.) Commit these three tenets to memory, and you'll be taking your first big step toward legendary greatness.

Bitches and divas are not the same thing.
Do not use the two words interchangeably, or I will cut you. Just kidding. That was a bitchy thing to say. See how I did that? Bitchiness comes from a place of insecurity, but being a diva comes from a place of strength and love. When you're a diva, you know deep down, regardless of what anyone else says about you, that you're beautiful. You also know that if you live in a place of light

and generosity, rather than in fear or darkness, good things will come to you. So, when a diva calls people on their bullshit—and, honey, you know how much we love to do this—we do it out of love. Tough love, yes, but it's still love, because unlike with a nasty bitch, other people's success and happiness do not threaten us. They inspire us. There's always room for more joy for me, for you, for everyone.

Divas expect others to do them, not do* for *them.
While divas make everything they do look easy, they actually work harder than anyone else. Behind all the glamour is always grit. And once you've got the determination and the do-whatever-it-takes work ethic instilled in you, it will never leave you. Being the kind of diva I'm talking about isn't about demanding all the green M&M's be plucked from your snack bowl in your dressing room. It's about staying late, trying harder, and working whatever you've got. My divas get shit done while staying true to who they are. Once you master that lesson, you can apply it to every aspect of your life, and you'll look and feel hotter for it.

All divas, no matter what size, sex, race, orientation, class, or fashion sense, are beautiful.
Like it or not, looks do matter in this world, and learning to work yours can be incredibly empowering. But that said, a true diva knows there's more to life than glue-on lashes and red lips. You already know—or at least you know you're supposed to know— that beauty comes from the inside, but to be a diva, you've got to

get to the point where you actually unquestioningly believe that. You can spend hours and a ton of money perfecting your flawless face and sick body, but if you don't have the personality or the sense of humor to back it up, then you're focusing on the wrong damn things. An ugly personality always trumps a beautiful face. Always. And anyone who doesn't know that isn't a diva. She's just an asshole with an attitude.

RULE *no.* 2:

BE THANKFUL YOU'RE A MISFIT.

If you are at all interesting, and honey, we already know you are because you're holding this book in your hands, you have probably at one time or another felt alone, or somehow different from everyone around you. Maybe you sing show tunes; maybe you wear assless chaps. Whatever your particular passion, if it's not football and beer or Pilates and Pinterest, your people may sometimes seem few and far between. But, if you live long enough (watch it!) you will learn a thing or two about being different. Namely, it is that very difference that will make you beautiful.

People often ask me how I got to be the only lady in a room of Ladyboys and the only heterosexual mother in a room of Muthas. It's because, like many of you, when I'm on the margins, I feel most at home. I've always been different, but to really understand just how different, you need to know where I came from.

Think of everything you know about what it is to be cool, and then understand that, as a kid, I was the exact opposite of whatever's in your head. I was never exactly "normal", which meant I never felt like I really belonged. I mean, while all the other kids tap-danced or did lame magic tricks in our second-grade talent show at John E. Riley Elementary, I took center stage and sang "Rhinestone Cowboy," accompanying myself on the f*cking organ. No joke. I played . . . AN ORGAN. I'm not so sure about the applause in the auditorium, but I swear to you, when I finished, the applause in my head went on for-evah.

My parents were always in the front row of my childhood performances, clapping the loudest and longest. They loved me more than I could ever possibly put into words. My dad Marty, who was raised as an Orthodox Jew in Baltimore, was a prankster, the type of guy who, every Halloween, would sit his rotund ass in the bathroom, holding a cheap RadioShack microphone, and watch out the window for trick-or-treaters. When they stepped onto our porch, he'd make the woodpile and a pumpkin talk and the kids would howl in surprise and delight. We were always the most popular house on October 31. He met and fell in love with my mom, Arlene, when she was just sixteen. My mom was a five-foot-tall, Brooklyn-born Jewish woman with a big mouth and an even bigger presence. She was a kind and passionate woman who wasn't afraid to use her voice. If she was happy, or even slightly annoyed by anything, anyone within in earshot of our house knew it. For instance, she had a love/hate relationship with our family dog. Every night, it was the same shrill chorus: "Get that damn dog out of the house!" and "Keep that damn dog quiet!" As a toddler, I was picking up words left and right, and so, having heard those two so often, I picked up one of my first-ever catchphrases:

"Damn dog." I said it all the time. Half proud, half mortified, my parents started calling the damn dog "DD" for short. (So, if you've ever wondered where my pipes—and my vulgarity—came from, you can thank Arlene, RIP.)

My parents waited until the moment my mom was of legal age and then got hitched. They spent many disappointing years trying to conceive and finally decided to adopt. I was the lucky baby they plucked out of a foster home. From the moment they took me in, when I was just about three months old, I was theirs and they were mine. Three years later, they adopted my brother, David. As I grew up, although we were a really tight-knit family, I had a sense that, just as I was different from the kids in my school, I was different from my parents too. At least physically. Perhaps the most bothersome difference came when I hit puberty and didn't get my mother's massive tits, which were all I'd wanted.

Now, I don't know if you've always felt like an outsider, but I don't even remember a time when I didn't know I was one. My parents explained to me that I was adopted as soon as I could understand. I remember them handing me a picture book called something like, *You Are an Adopted Child*. Honestly, I was more disappointed with the title of that book than I was with the message. I mean, could no one do better? I would've much preferred it be called *Your Parents Didn't Love You Enough to Keep You*, or even *So, You Look Like No One in Your Family*. My high school boyfriend would later tease me by saying my parents won me on the quarter wheel on the Wildwood boardwalk, and the jokes just went on and on and on, usually coming from my dad, which is where I get my relentless, wicked, twisted sense of humor. It ain't always genetic, kids, sometimes it's about your environment, and for that, I am grateful.

Fast forward to my midtwenties, when my music career had stalled (more on that later). I needed to figure out what to do with my life next. But to move forward, the first thing I needed to do was look back. I needed to know where I came from to know where I was headed next. So, I started tracking down my birth parents. My mother, Arlene, even helped me, at first begrudgingly and then enthusiastically. Her attitude changed when her sister, my aunt Harriet, said to her, "Listen, Arlene. You can be upset, but the way I see it, you should be kissing this woman's feet for doing what she did, because if she hadn't, we wouldn't have our Michelle." Like so many things in life, it's all about perception. Remember that, my divas.

The first time I heard my birth mother's voice, it all just clicked. I was twenty-five years old and I had to jump through some hoops with the adoption agency for them to take the next steps and attempt to locate her. I had to consent to meeting with their in-house therapist, which I did, and after she saw me mentally fit to continue, they were the ones who would do the heavy lifting. When the agency finally located her through social security, after her driver's license provide to be a dead end, they called me to tell me they had found her and she was very eager to speak to me. They asked me if I wanted to call her or if she should call me. I immediately said that I wanted her to call me. When my phone rang, it was like the world had stopped turning. I knew

I have always been drawn to big balls.

THE

PEOPLE SPEND A LOT OF TIME TRYING TO FIT IN, hoping to be accepted, because they think fitting in will make them feel "normal." But it doesn't make you normal. It makes you average, and average is something a diva never wants to be. You are anything but average, and if you can remember that, you can approach the world from a place of strength, rather than weakness. So even if you feel like a misfit, be thankful for it. It's what makes you stand out from the crowd.

THE

DIVA
RULES

Ditch the Drama, Find Your Strength,
and Sparkle Your Way to the Top

BY MICHELLE VISAGE

Foreword by RUPAUL

CHRONICLE BOOKS
SAN FRANCISCO

Library of Congress Cataloging-in-Publication Data

Visage, Michelle.
  The diva rules : ditch the drama, find your strength, and sparkle
your way to the top / by Michelle Visage.
     pages cm
  Summary: "A humorous book of advice by Michelle Visage"--
Provided by publisher.
  ISBN 978-1-4521-4232-6 (hardback)
1. Success. 2. Conduct of life. I. Title.

  BJ1611.2.V575 2015
  650.1--dc23

                        2015012770

Manufactured in Canada.

Design by Michael Morris
Jacket Photograph by Mathu Andersen
Makeup and Styling by Sutan (Raja) Amrull
Hair by Hector Pocasangre

10 9 8 7 6 5 4 3 2

Chronicle Books LLC
680 Second Street
San Francisco, CA 94107
www.chroniclebooks.com

Chronicle books and gifts are available at special quantity discounts
to corporations, professional associations, literacy programs, and
other organizations. For details and discount information,
please contact our premiums department at corporatesales@
chroniclebooks.com or at 1-800-759-0190.

TO ALL OF MY CHILDREN, YOUNG AND EXPERIENCED,
MAY YOU ALLOW YOUR INNER DIVA TO SHINE
LIKE THE STARS YOU ARE.

CONTENTS

FOREWORD BY
RuPaul
p. 8

INTRODUCTION: p. 13

RULE *no.* 1

Live by
THE THREE TENETS
of divahood.

p. 17

RULE *no.* 2

Be thankful
you're a
misfit.

p. 20

RULE *no.* 3

**YOU HAVE
A VOICE.**
Use it.

p. 26

RULE *no.* 4

Get off
your ass,
girl.

p. 32

RULE *no.* 5

*Find your
scene.*

p. 47

RULE *no.* 6

Give good face.

p. 53

RULE *no.* 7

You do you.

p. 60

RULE *no.* 8

Keep your
shit together.

p. 66

RULE *no.* 9

Be the honey
and
**WAIT FOR
THE BEES.**

p. 73

RULE *no.* 10

*Celebrate
your
competition.*

p. 79

RULE *no.* 11

*Believe you're
the best*
(*or* **FAKE IT UNTIL
YOU ARE.**)

p. 93

RULE *no.* 12

*Exposure
isn't money,*
**BUT SOMETIMES
IT CAN BE WORTH
MORE.**

p. 99

RULE *no.* 13

*Never give up
on yourself.*
NE-VER.

p. 108

it was her, and as soon as I picked up, everything just started pouring out of both of us. Joanne was living in Murfreesboro, Tennessee, and her Jersey accent had taken on a soft Southern twang. She's Irish-Hungarian Catholic, and she got knocked up the moment she lost her virginity at nineteen years old to a guy named Lewis, who just went by Wiss. (Apparently, as a child, he couldn't pronounce his full name, and this shorter version stuck throughout his entire life.) I remember saying to her, probably way too early in the conversation, "Oh my God, why do I have no boobs?" because yes, darling, the world does revolve around my tits. I went on, "Why do I have a bump on my nose? Who was my father? Tell me *everything*." And she did, and I ate up every word.

The next week, I was on a plane to Nashville to meet her, as well as her verbally abusive, alcoholic boyfriend, whom I hated instantly because of the way he spoke to her, but I digress. Now, with a situation like meeting your birth mother, you never know how these things are going to go. She met me at the airport, and when I saw her, we hugged, but it wasn't this grand moment where the heavens above opened and a beam of light shone upon us. We had no mother/daughter connection at all—zero—because I already had a mom. I didn't know how I was going to feel, but in that moment, I didn't feel anything but grateful—grateful to know where I'd come from and grateful to be able to say thank you. And I did. Now that I am a mother I am even more grateful to Joanne for what she did, especially when you take in account that she was nineteen years old. She gave me the opportunity to have a great life because she knew she couldn't, and to me? That's the most selfless act of all.

RULE _no._ 3:

YOU HAVE A VOICE. USE IT.

Divas, whatever you do in life, or whatever you want to do in life, the one thing you have to do first is to get noticed. And you can't get noticed if you never speak up. You have a voice, honey, and it's good for more than singing show tunes in the shower, yelling at the TV during _RuPaul's Drag Race_ (Monday nights on Logo TV, or online at logotv.com, *ting*), or gossiping with your friends about the Duchess of Windsor. Whether your voice comes in the form of song, dance, fashion, art, or being a friggin' mime for all I care, you need to learn to project, darling, and show the world who you are. Take center stage. Sparkle, Neely, sparkle.

You already know that my mom Arlene gave me my voice. But before we can get to the part about how I took to the stage and screen and became FABULOUS, I need to tell you about how Belinda Carlisle, my first true love, taught me how to use my voice. Before her, I guess you could say, I did not have the beat.

I was a radio-obsessed kid, and I'm fully aware of how stupid this sounds, but during the summer before seventh grade, when I was in the full throes of my chubby awkward phase, the Go-Gos saved my life. I was different from the kids at school, different from my family, different from the Jews, different from the non-Jews, and here was this all-girl group, which, for the first time in my life, immediately made me feel like a part of something bigger than myself. When I heard "Our Lips Are Sealed," and later "We Got the Beat," I felt connected to them and to the world. They were like me, and I was like them. And Belinda Carlisle, who was thick and curvy and gorgeous, also wore a miniskirt! I literally became obsessed with her. I wanted to feel that free, that powerful. She made me feel like, for the first time, it was OK to be myself.

Belinda and her all-girl band helped me discover fashion, which became my main form of self-expression. My new uniform was unlike any other sixth grader's in South Plainfield, New Jersey, and it always involved miniskirts and white Keds covered in felt-tip-markered lightning bolts. By the seventh grade I started getting heavily into punk rock music and even gave myself a mohawk (inspired by the sexy Annabella from Bow Wow Wow, though when I emerged from my bathroom after my self-styled hair-don't, Arlene was *not* amused). Dyeing it blue was the pinnacle for me—thank *God* my parents were cool and knew it was a phase, albeit a pretty long one. The summer between eighth and ninth grades was a huge one for me as we took a family trip to England. My first trip abroad and I literally fell in love. England was the birthplace of punk rock and the home of the Sex Pistols and William Shakespeare alike. Heaven.

THE

THOSE EARLY LESSONS that I learned on that football field in New Jersey have stayed with me my whole life. And now, when I look at these kids on *RuPaul's Drag Race*, doing their own big reveals, I see myself, because I remember what it felt like to learn how to use my authentic voice. When you live your life in the audience, you start to seek approval from the other people in it, and then you become a giant, predictable bore. But when you're courageous enough to stand in front of the crowd, and really speak up, you become more powerful. And if you can do that, you'll never be part of the chorus of someone else's show. Instead, you'll always be the lead diva in your own musical.

My mom and dad really went out of their way spending hard-earned wages on my shopping sprees through all of the markets London, provided for better or for worse. I returned to New Jersey a changed teen in many ways, but fashion was a big one. I was really into wearing spiked necklaces, bracelets, and belts, so much so that the kids started calling me "Spike." I was *everything*, but nobody knew what to make of me.

In school in the eighties, all the kids fell into different cliques. You had your jocks, your burnouts, the band geeks, the A/V club, and the cool kids, which included the cheerleaders. In South Plainfield, we also had the black kids and the white kids who acted like black kids. I got along with everyone, but belonged nowhere. I was a punk rock theater geek who played sax in the marching band. No one ever gave me a second look until, I swear to you, I sang Liza Minnelli's version of "New York, New York" (look it up) in the sixth-grade talent show. Then I became The Girl with the Voice, the girl who could sing, and it gave me confidence in myself. I never cared about cliques. All I cared about was being talented and funny, which is why I eventually earned the title of class clown (Or shall I say class humorist, because clowns felt offended by the title. Don't believe me? Look it up: South Plainfield High School class of '86).

By my senior year, I'd become captain and choreographer for the pom-pom squad, which is not to be confused with the cheerleading squad. I couldn't give a shit about sports. We were responsible for the halftime show at the football games, and I wanted to make ours the best spectacle the school had ever seen. And let me tell you, honey, it was, and still to this day is, the best thing the people of South Plainfield have ever witnessed. Because when I was captain, rather than go out and make pointless pyramids on the fifty-yard line, we did—are you ready?—a full-on striptease, complete with a big reveal at the end. We made gloves that were green on one side and white on the other, colors I still regret, but for the finale, we ripped off our skirts, which we'd cut and Velcroed back together, to reveal our gold-sequined panties underneath. I was doing drag moves before I knew what drag even was!

RULE no. 4:

GET OFF YOUR ASS, GIRL.

I know you have a dream. Guess what? Everybody does. And I know you're special, but guess what? Everybody is. I'm not being mean here. I'm just giving it to you straight. You've got some fierce competition out there. And the single most important factor that's going to determine whether or not you actually make your dream come true, whatever it may be, is not your talent. It's your tenacity and your willingness to work harder than anyone else to get what you want. You don't become a diva by sitting at home, watching Golden Girls reruns. If you want to be golden, girl, you've got to get out there and make a name for yourself, because let me tell you, nobody else is going to make it for you. You can't buy your way into the corner office or onto the cover of *Vogue*. You have to earn it. I learned that lesson the hard way.

When I graduated from South Plainfield High, I had big dreams. I wanted to be a Broadway star, and in case that didn't work out, I was smart enough to have a backup plan. I'd just become a movie star instead. I had the talent. I could sing and I could act. My audition tapes were so hot that despite my B-minus average I won full scholarships to join the theater

My gap was so huge, my mom told me to smile with my mouth closed.

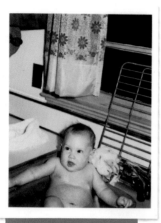

My boobs literally never grew any bigger than this . . .

What camera? Where?

I always knew the power of a great ass.

My brother David and I wearing Arlene couture. She made our clothes.

Mother-made or not, fashion has always been important to me.

3-70

Clowns are my biggest fear and this is where it started. Made by Arlene, of course.

Marty and Arlene when they were teens. The best parents a girl could hope for.

My idea of a hiding place. It never seemed to work.

Happiness in the '70s: a poncho and an anti-childproofed swing set in your backyard.

My favorite dressy outfit back then . . . and it was green. I *loved* a go-go boot.

Mom's prized possessions: her Hummels and her kids.

My home, the stage. I was Liesl with the harshest Jersey accent. It was heaven.

Nothing says Jersey Shore like a black and white bikini and a perm.

This was the outfit I chose to sing to my dad for his surprise fiftieth. Extremely under-stated and demure, no?

My first serious rock band, White Lightning. Adam Ant tee and dolphin shorts. Yes.

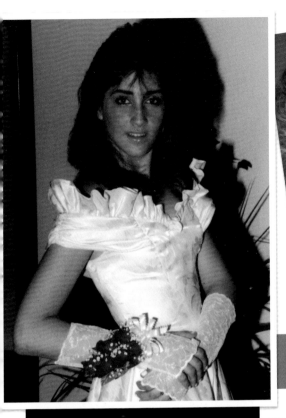

My hair was so big it didn't even fit in my driver's license picture. Hidden from the shot was my boyfriend's giant nameplate that read simply: TONY.

Sophomore year going to the junior prom with my first boyfriend, Glenn. Madonna had nothing on these lace gloves.

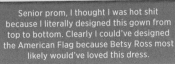

My boyfriend Michael gave me his jacket because I was cold. This was right before I found out he was late picking me up because he was getting a BJ from the tux rental girl.

Senior prom, I thought I was hot shit because I literally designed this gown from top to bottom. Clearly I could've designed the American Flag because Betsy Ross most likely would've loved this dress.

My most conservative portrait ever: my senior picture. I did this only for Arlene. I mean, pearls? *Who* was I kidding?

programs at a handful of solid schools: NYU, Syracuse, Ithaca, Rutgers. But rather than go to any of these esteemed institutions, I decided I didn't want to have to deal with the English lit classes and biology labs that are part of a well-rounded liberal arts education. Instead, I made the asinine decision to attend the American Musical and Dramatic Academy in New York City, which, at the time, was an unaccredited joke of a college, offering two-year, good-for-nothing associate's degrees, which in all honesty were basically just certificates. (FYI: it has since changed to an actual accredited college.) It was also so expensive that my parents had to take out a second mortgage on their house to pay the tuition. Now, I don't believe in regret. If you spend your whole life looking in the rearview mirror, you're going to crash. But Jesus, Mary, Joseph, and Ru, I have a hard time with that one, and I think everyone else does as well. Shout-out to AMDA class of '88.

If I squint really hard and try to think of a silver lining to my terrible decision, I can come up with two: The first is that I had one tough lady for a speech teacher, and she taught me how to lose my ridiculous accent. I was a Jersey girl raised by a Brooklyn mother, so just imagine that for minute. Everything was "Let's have 'cawwfeee' and 'tawwwk' about the 'dawwwg.'" My teacher, Barbara Adrian, taught me to practice my speech with a cork in my mouth, and I worked on my pronunciation every single day for two years until my accent was gone (or at least as close to gone as it was ever going to get). The second bright spot: I was in New York City. To me, that was the center of the world, home to

Broadway, casting directors, and my favorite fashion designers, especially Betsey Johnson and Patricia Field. It was also a place where I knew I could be free to be myself without anyone looking at me like I was a freak.

My look when I arrived to NYC was full-on guidette. Think Meadow Soprano with a disco twist. I'd abandoned my punk rock aesthetic when I started hitting the teen clubs and I decided to take it up a notch by frosting my hair and tanning until I was the color of a Louis Vuitton speedy bag. The teen clubs were now my oasis, and I quite literally ruled the roost. My daily schedule went something like this: school, *General Hospital*, homework, club prep, magic time. My mom, bless her, usually dropped me off. Teen clubs had become my obsession starting at around age fifteen and also a source of newfound uber popularity, but college awaited. As the date of my move to New York City approached, I was practically sick with the twisted cocktail of excitement for the future and regret over missing out on the New Jersey teen club scene.

I was seventeen years old when my parents dropped me off at the Hotel Beacon on Seventy-fifth and Broadway, which is where I lived during college. And though I'd been coming to New York with my mom twice a year since junior high to buy cheap knock-offs on Canal Street, I was terrified to be left alone. For the first three months of school, I didn't walk farther than a block away from my room, certain that if I ventured beyond that radius, I'd be jumped, mugged, or raped, probably by a homeless person. I was scared shitless of everyone and everything, especially the subway, and my fear made The Big City real small, real fast.

I called my mom every single day, and on the first two weekends of school, I bucked up enough to take the train home from Penn Station, all alone, to South Plainfield to hit my usual circuit of Jersey teen clubs. On the third weekend, I called my mom to tell her what time to pick me up from the train station, and she told me she wouldn't do it. "You can't come home anymore," she said. I threw a complete toddler temper tantrum on the phone. I was pissed off, sad, and confused, but she wasn't having any of it. "You moved to New York City to become a star, and you're not going to find anything more for yourself in Jersey," she said. "Go to the clubs in NYC, meet people, network!" I said, "Ma! I don't know anybody here. I'm eighteen. I don't even know how to get into a club!" But that was the end of our conversation, and I spent that weekend, sulking in my dorm room.

A few days later, a postmarked envelope from my dear old mom showed up at my dorm. Inside, there was a note that said, "This should help, sweetie," and attached to it was a fake ID and a fraudulent birth certificate, which she even had notarized. To this day, I have no idea how she got hold of these scam documents, since there was no Internet back then, but I imagine she found an ad for them in the back of *MAD* magazine and sent my passport photo and twenty-five bucks off to some pimply kid who ran an operation out of the paneled basement of his parents' house. She never worried about me becoming a raging teenage alcoholic, because I never drank (and still don't to this day). My new red-and-white fake ID stated that I was a twenty-one-year-old student named Michelle Shupack attending the University of Texas. Now, I had no excuses.

I knew I had to start getting myself out there. My two roommates, Jolie from Marietta, Georgia, and Dana from Swankytown, Connecticut, already had agents and alleged Broadway

THE

T

IF YOU REALLY WANT SOMETHING, YOU HAVE TO GO OUT AND GET IT YOURSELF. I know how frustrating it can be when you don't even know where to start, or can't even get your foot in the door for an interview, an audition, a date, whatever. But, repeat after me: Do. Not. Give. Up. Put yourself out there: Go online, ask everyone you know, and don't feel shy about it either. You're just looking for a lead, not a handout. Every interaction you have is a new opportunity, so don't waste it by sitting on your ass. Start with things so small that you think they'll probably be worthless. Put yourself where you know the people with power congregate—at the bar, the café, the restaurant, the pool, the charity—and get yourself noticed. Even tiny things can lead to something bigger. And don't ever, ever count on anybody else to do the work for you. It's all on you, and that's as it should be. Because if you don't earn your success yourself, I guarantee that it's not going to last. You've got to work it to get it, and then you've got to work it to keep it. If you can remember that, you'll do just fine.

connections, because their families had money. I had to become my own agent. Every week, I'd read through a theater newspaper called *Backstage*, which announced open casting calls, and as I became more comfortable living in the city, I started going to all of them. They were cattle calls, and I'd often stand in lines that wrapped around the block for hours only to hear the casting director come out and announce, "Thank you very much, but we've filled the part," before I even got within a block of the door. I only ever got one booking from an open call. I was signed by a modeling agency called Judith's Petites, but it turned out to be a scam. I should've known. Who the hell hires a petite model? No one. That's who.

I knew my city-smart mom, thanks to her Brooklyn childhood, was right about the clubs. Everything that seemed to be happening in New York was happening downtown. Deejays such as Junior Vasquez, David Morales, and Frankie Knuckles were suddenly becoming world-famous, and since I couldn't get my foot into the stage door, I decided that the club door would have to do.

One day, I'd heard some kids at school talking about this club called The Underground off Union Square, and I recruited my drama-school bestie, Aurea, to go there with me one night. It must've been eleven o'clock when we arrived, and there was this massive bouncer at the door perched on a stool in a black leather jacket. I was so scared when I approached him that my hands were literally shaking. Anybody who laid eyes on me (and my white-frosted hair) would've known instantly that I was a Jersey girl (in NYC we were called the "Bridge and Tunnel" crowd, and we were not the favored elite). The moment I opened my mouth, the Jersey shore poured out. I came prepared, though, having memorized everything about my new identity: "Howdy! I'm twenty-one, a Gemini, from Podunk, Texas. Oh yeah, I love UT. Go Longhorns! And if you don't believe me, here's my birth certificate, pardner." Despite my obvious fraud, the bouncer, who, like all bouncers in the city, would later become my friend, got a kick out of me and let me in. Aurea and I quickly made our way down the narrow stairs, past the coat-check girl, and into this cavernous room where the bass was pumping, and so were the bodies. I had arrived. And it was there, in those dark, sweaty, legendary dance halls at The Underground, as well as the Palladium, the Copa, the World, and Tracks, that I started working it every night, and where I made all the connections that would lead me to where I am today.

In a sense, going to the clubs became my job. Even if none of my friends wanted to go with me, I'd go by myself, because I wasn't there to party. I was there to get noticed. By the end of my first semester, I dropped my guidette look and transformed myself into a wild drag child. I went for sexy all the time. My uniform: leggings, combat boots, a black bra, and hair extensions. The long blond ponytail was part of my signature look. And trust me, there were some nights when I would've rather stayed home and watched *21 Jump Street*, but I knew if I wanted to make a name for myself, I couldn't do it on my futon in the Hotel Beacon.

RULE *no.* 5:

FIND YOUR SCENE.

Every single day I get emails from people all over the world, and there's always at least one from someone who feels lost or lonely. They feel like they don't fit in or like they have no community or like they'll always be kept down, simply because they don't follow the unwritten rules of how they should look (boring) or act (boring). And you know what? I write back to every single one of those sweet souls, because I know in my heart what it feels like to be completely surrounded by people and yet still feel lonely. I know that ache. And here's what I say to them (and to you and to my own daughters too): If you're not liking the people around you, it's up to you to change your surroundings and find new people. And keep an open mind, because you never know who will become your next BFF.

Take me, for example: The underground queer scene of New York City doesn't exactly sound like home for a straight, white, teenaged female drama nerd from Jersey, but after I moved to Manhattan at the tender age of seventeen, it soon became mine. When my parents dropped me off at my hotel-room-turned-dorm at the Hotel Beacon on the Upper West Side, I didn't know a single one of the eight million people who lived in the city. I'd hoped to meet some kindred spirits at my drama school, but unfortunately, I learned within the first few weeks that my particular college drew more former-pageant-queen types than future-drag-queen types. I was a foul-mouthed, tough-talking Jersey girl among Southern belles and socialites, and after my mom forbade me to come home, I felt more alone than ever.

And then I was rescued. Or maybe I should say, I got myself rescued, because I wasn't just bobbing around, waiting for someone to come and be my friend. I went out searching for like-minded people, and on my first night at The Underground, I found them. I was there in that dark, crowded club to get noticed, so I was dancing my little ass off to Janet Jackson, Information Society, Rob Base, and whatever thumping house/freestyle music the DJ spun. Having spent nearly every single night of my high school years in the teen clubs in New Jersey, I had moves that could put the *Solid Gold* dancers to shame, and I was seriously throwing down when this queen named David approached. He leaned into my ear and yelled over the music, "Girl, you are fierce! What's your name?" I told him. We danced together for a song or two, and then, he grabbed my hand and led me through the gyrating, sweaty masses into this back room, where he introduced me to the biggest group of misfits I'd ever had the privilege to behold. Boys, girls, straight, gay, black, white—they all had their hair straightened and shellacked with so much Aqua Net that it looked like they had LP records resting at a 45-degree angle on their heads. Then, "Love is a Message" by MFSB came on and, as if on cue, they all started doing something I'd never seen before in my entire life. I froze. My jaw was on the floor. I could hardly breathe. They were Vogueing. What was it? To put it in layman's terms: Vogueing is a campy, stylized version of runway modeling that has flourished for decades in Harlem and made its way main-stream through gay nightlife.

"What is that? I want to try it!" I squealed, giddy at the sight of them. And I watched and learned, and they taught me, and then every night I'd go home to my dorm room and practice more in front of my mirror, where my two prissy roommates would sneer at me, "What the hell are you doing?" Honestly, I wasn't even exactly sure myself, but I knew I loved it, and even more, I knew I wanted to be a part of this magnificent group of freaks. Among them were two legends: Cesar Valentino, the now-famous choreographer, who became not only my dance mentor but also one of my best friends; and Willi Ninja, who, upon his death in 2006, would be called "The Grandfather of Vogue" by the *New York Times*.

From The Underground, we branched out into other clubs: the World, the Palladium, Tracks. Those long, sweaty nights of dancing would almost always include Vogue battles, where everyone would circle up and two dancers would walk into the center to compete. I was good, and I knew it, because the legends not only told me so, they also taught me all of my moves. So I'd strut into those circles and face off, usually against some fierce femme queens, who were ladyboys or transitioning girls. I'm not lying when I tell you this: I never lost a single battle. Never. I ruled those competitions, and eventually I was featured on the nightly news and won a dance contest with Cesar on a TV show called *The Latin Connection*, where we introduced Vogueing to America (and also, I guess, to Madonna, but that's another story).

Until this point, I could count on one hand the number of gay people I'd met in my life. There was Glen, the dandy, who was bullied in high school. And then there was this one punk-rock Jewish girl who got me drunk on Everclear and seduced me in her car in the parking lot at JFTY (Jewish Federation of Temple Youth) dance when I was a junior in high school. (Yeah, I went, I just didn't stay inside.) Cesar, Willi, David, and my other friend, Max, introduced me not only to a new kind of dance but also to a world unlike any I'd ever known. We started hanging out all the time, and when we weren't in the clubs, we would meet up on the piers that dotted the Hudson River in the West Village.

The pier culture was unlike anything I've ever experienced in my life, and it's where I learned everything I know about gay culture and gay history. I remember one night, leaning on the railing with Mother Angie Xtravaganza, who was one of the first trans girls I ever met, learning all about her family, her children. Most of these kids came from nothing. Many were homeless, not by cruel acts of God but by crueler acts of their parents (or, more often, parent or maybe just grandmother), who kicked them out for being queer. With no money to speak of (and despite the growing AIDS crisis), many would turn tricks in order to get by—and smoke dust in order to forget.

THE

T

YOUR FRIENDS MAY NOT BE WHO YOU EXPECT THEM TO BE. Look at me: I wanted to be a Broadway actor, so when I moved to New York, I thought I was going to be hanging with other theater people, not the world's most fabulous poor homeless kids on the piers and in the clubs. But if I'd closed myself off to them, just because they weren't in line with my expectations, I would have missed out on some of the most meaningful friendships of my life. If you haven't found your home yet, know that you do have one out there. You just have to look for it. You have to put yourself out there in order to make new friends, and that can be scary, but there's no getting around it. Go to parties. Ask a coworker out for drinks or coffee. If you're a churchgoer, or Kabbalah follower, or a freaking Jedi knight, get involved with your house of worship. If you like to dance, go to clubs or classes. If you like to cook, hang out in the cookbook aisle at Barnes & Noble and start talking to people there. You won't look like a creep if you chat somebody up in a bookstore, especially if you're holding my book in your hand. Ting! Wherever you go, you've just got to open your mouth and talk. If you go out but speak to no one, what's the point? Besides, most people are not going to be rude to you for introducing yourself, and if they are, screw them. You don't want them in your life anyway. Act the way you'd like your friends to act, and I promise they will come to you and you will find the love you deserve.

Of course, that wasn't me. I was blessed with a loving, middle-class family, and yet I always felt different. And perhaps sensing that I had no other place to go, these gorgeous, sparkly, fabulous, open-hearted queens on the piers and in the clubs took me in, not even just as a friend, but as one of them. They became my surrogate family. Almost everybody in these gay clubs at the time was part of a "house," essentially an acquired family made up of a mother, usually a drag queen, a very femme man, or a trans woman; a father, who was often more butch; and about twenty to thirty children. My closest friends, were in the house known as The Magnifiques, and my BFF/mentor Cesar, was the father of the house. There were many other houses and some of the major players were (and still are): The Xtravaganzas, who were the most fabulous and everyone wanted to be a part of; The Ninjas, of which I was an honorary member; the House of Pendavis, where my baby Jerome was the house's legendary Voguer; the House of La Beija, and dozens more. I never questioned them and they never questioned me. We just knew we loved each other and belonged together. Someone would bring a boom box, and we'd Vogue on the Hudson as the giant freighters and their tugboats passed by. We'd sit around on the railings having reading sessions, where we'd all spit truths at each other for entertainment. *This* is where I learned to throw serious shade. It's where I mastered my side-eye, a look that even today carries even more weight than words. And every night, all night, we'd just hang together, arm in arm, and kiki. And it was there, under the light of the moon, where I'd finally found my people and my place in the world. I was home.

RULE _no._ 6:

GIVE GOOD FACE.

This may come as a shocker to you, or maybe it'll just be a relief: No diva feels beautiful every single moment of every single day. I don't care if you're Gisele and your legs are five miles long, there will be times when self-doubt creeps into your psyche and just clobbers the shit out of you. Believe me, I've been there. And what's so maddening about that split second when your self-confidence just up and vanishes is that it's so often triggered by something so small and stupid: a zit, frizzy hair, an unflattering picture, a stumble, or the feeling that you have nothing decent to wear. Divas, you cannot let those silly little saboteurs wreck you. Do not give up and hand over your power so easily. Instead, dig your acrylics in—break one if you must, *gasp*—and hang on with all of your might to this real and unchangeable truth: You are beautiful as you are. You woke up like that. And once you understand that simple truth, you don't have to be scared of letting your true face, your true emotions, your true self show. And that's giving good face.

I never knew that I was beautiful when I was growing up. Hell, I couldn't get a boy's attention if my life depended on it (and from the sixth grade on I tried, I mean realllllly tried). I felt invisible. After I moved to New York City upon graduation and became friends with the queens in the clubs, my attitude toward myself began to change. They simply loved me for my natural look: my cheekbones, my skin, my green eyes, even the crazy bump on my nose. It was a total and complete revelation to me. I could be beautiful just by being me. And with that discovery and their support, my confidence grew by leaps and bounds.

Believing I was gorgeous is what made me so fierce. It's part of what gave me the confidence to enter into Vogue battles against any other queen who dared to step up against me. It allowed me to open myself up to other people for the first time, because I no longer felt threatened by anyone else. And please don't get me wrong here. I'm not saying I felt better or prettier than anyone else. I didn't think that, and I still sure as hell don't. I'm saying that when I realized I had beauty to offer just by being me, I also understood that everyone else did too. We were all freaks, geeks, and weird, wild messes, and we all bared our hearts (and often way more than that) in those clubs. We were in this together, dancing, loving, living, and sometimes just barely surviving. The beauty of it all was spectacular. I spent most of my time with the Magnifiques. When we weren't downtown dancing in the clubs or hanging on the piers, we were way, way, way uptown in Harlem, competing in what were known as "balls." They were part beauty pageant, part dance competition, part fashion show, and all party.

Before I ever went to my first ball, my crew thoroughly schooled me on what to expect. When a ball was scheduled, usually once a month, the host family would post flyers on the walls outside of the clubs downtown to alert other houses. On the flyers, they'd list the categories of the competition, and then each house would meet together in someone's apartment in order to prepare for the event. This was always an issue for me, since most of the Magnifiques lived in Spanish Harlem, and I was already terrified to travel above Eightieth Street, let alone into Harlem. Even if I had the money for a cab, none of the cabbies wanted to venture into those parts of town, so I had no choice but to brave the train . . . alone. Anyway, at our monthly meetings, we'd plan who would walk which category and what costumes each of us would have to sew. The categories would include titles such as Femme Queen Realness, Butch Queen First Time in Heels, European Runway, Face with a Flaw, Vogueing, and dozens more. The biggest sin you could make at a ball (and, I'd argue, also in life) was to be boring, so we held nothing back.

My first ball was hosted by the Xtravaganzas, a family made up of the most fabulous queens in the city. Based on their attitudes, they knew they had it going on too. Everybody, including me, secretly wanted to be an Xtravaganza. The balls would begin around eleven o'clock at night in a random rental hall somewhere in the five boroughs, depending on the house. Like at a debutante or royal ball, each house was announced upon its entrance, so the

Magnifiques would meet outside at a corner bodega or another nearby place so we could all walk in, hand in hand, and make a dramatic entrance together. Family.

There had to have been several hundred queens at this ball, most of them black or Latino and all of them fierce. There was a makeshift runway in the center of the room, and at the end of the runway was the Holy Grail: the judges' table. The judges were usually prominent figures in the community: house mothers or fathers and sometimes even a local journalist such as Michael Musto. An announcer would call the categories and name the competitors, and a DJ would play music, usually off someone's borrowed boom box. Each competitor would walk not only for a title, but also a trophy, a giant golden monument of plastic that bestowed bragging rights on its holder. If you snatched a trophy, you were officially the shit. After a certain amount of trophies, you achieved the ultimate status: Legendary.

I had no plans to walk in that first ball, or any ball really. I was there to be supportive and for the fun and the experience. I spent most of that night taking it all in and cheering for all the queens from the sidelines. But when the announcer called the Vogue category, Cesar literally put his hands behind my back, shoved me out onto the runway, and yelled, "Get the f*ck out there now!" And so I did. I Vogued my ass off just as I had so many nights in the clubs. It was the scariest, most exhilarating moment of my life, and everyone in that hall was screaming for me, Michelle Magnifique. I was the first biological woman ever to walk the Vogue category in a ball, and I killed it. When I snatched that trophy, everyone started hooting and hollering for me, this skinny white girl from Jersey. There was no shade, just love. Pure, open-armed love.

I competed in a few other balls after that one, and every time I walked in the Vogue category, I snatched that trophy. And soon, at the urging of the other Magnifiques, I branched out into another category known simply as "Face." But there was nothing simple about the Face category, as all the queens were beautiful. It became a battle of wits. You had to get the judges to look at YOU, not the other queens. If they spent too long looking at someone else, it meant they could fall in love with them and you would risk losing. Now, when you walk the Face category, it's because your face is flawless, though not by the dictionary definition, but by our definition in the community. It's all about your bone structure and skin. It's about walking the runway like a model, laying your face on the judges' table, and giving them the sort of pure beauty realness. When I walked the category, I'd cover my entire face with Pond's white cold cream, strut to the judges' table, dramatically take a white tissue out of somewhere in my barely there ensemble, and wipe off the cream in a grand gesture of, "Who needs makeup when their face is this flawless?" I won that category too.

Soon, all the Latin queens who knew me from the clubs and the balls started calling me "Cara," Spanish for "face," rolling the "R" off their tongues. "Cara, Cara! Come here, Cara!" Almost instantly, I left my God-given name behind and started going by my new queen-given moniker. Mirrored letters were every-

THE IF YOU WANT TO SUCCEED, YOU'VE GOT TO LEARN HOW TO GIVE GOOD FACE, and that doesn't mean you've got to be pretty. It means you've got to own who you are and what you've got, know that you're beautiful, and, baby, act like it. On *Drag Race*, I often critique these young queens by saying they're not showing enough of themselves. They hide behind the wigs and the makeup and the characters they play, fearful that if they reveal who they really are, they'll not be good enough, or likable enough. We all do that in life sometimes. When we're scared that we don't measure up, we hide behind things: excuses, other people, schticks, fake personas. But here's the thing: If you're constantly hiding behind something or someone else, life will pass you by. Opportunities will pass you by. Relationships will pass you by. Back in the ball scene, if you wanted to win the Face category, you had to be willing to strip yourself down, take everything off, and let your own best features shine through. The same holds true in life. If you want to win, you have to be willing to be vulnerable. Believe me, I know. That's what gave me my name, and ultimately, my power.

thing to every club kid at the time, thanks to Patricia Field. But since I could not afford her designs, I went to Pearl Art Supply and splurged on two Cs, four As, and two Rs, and then epoxied "CARA" on the back of my white leather motorcycle jacket and on the front of my baseball hat. Unfortunately, the white kids on the street would mess it up all the time. They'd yell, in their New York accents, "Hey, Cara!" as if it rhymed with Farrah, and I hated it.

Having taken six years of French, the international language of sexy, I changed Cara, which means "face" in Spanish, into Visage, which means "face" in French. I guess you could say it's my drag name, but I earned it not from putting on makeup to become someone else, but by taking it off to reveal myself. To this day, I do my damnedest to uphold the legacy of my name, Michelle Visage.

RULE <u>no.</u> 7:

YOU DO YOU.

I don't care who you are, everybody needs to feel loved. In fact, that desire is so strong in all of us that sometimes we're willing to do anything to get it, including becoming someone we're not. But here's the thing: If you start changing yourself—who you are, how you act, and what you care about—just to please other people, you will fail not only them but, more important, yourself.

Believe me, I know how easy it is to get sucked in. I'm a chameleon myself. When I went to England on vacation with my parents at age thirteen I returned with a British accent, which lasted most of the summer. And not even a sometimes British accent, like Madonna had when she was married to Guy Richie. Oh no, I was full-on *Downton Abbey*. On the opposite end of the spectrum, in high school, rap music was my life. It took over my soul the first time I heard Rapper's Delight as a child, in 1979. When I hung with fellow rap fans, who were usually the black kids of South Plainfield and Plainfield, I talked and acted just like them, because I was one of them. I was down. But my most dramatic transformation happened when I was eighteen and started hanging out with pier queens in New York City.

By the time I graduated from college, I was lucky enough to be living on the corner of Mulberry and Houston streets in a brand-spankin'-new, twenty-four-hour doorman building, in a one-bedroom apartment. I know that sounds flossy and pampered, but the catch was; I was sharing a one-bedroom apartment with two other girls. Yes, a tiny-ass, NYC apartment with ONE bedroom to be shared by three girls, nay, women. ONE BATHROOM, three twin beds in one bedroom—ya feel me? Looking back, it was a terrible decision, but it was the only way to live in the element we wanted and be able to afford it. Now, pretty much every single night of the week, I'd go to the clubs with my gays. They were my family. Max, Danny, Jeannie, Cesar, Fidel, David, Tony, Jerome Pendavis, and Princess, in particular, were my closest friends in the world. We spent every free moment together, and my apartment became the usual preclub gathering place. I'd be in the bathroom getting ready, and they'd be hanging out on my couch, playing mix tapes or watching TV. Then, we'd go to the clubs and dance our tiny little asses off. When the clock struck three, we'd tumble into Florent, a popular diner in the meatpacking district (my GOD, that neighborhood has the biggest double entendre of all!), which was not unlike being in the club itself, since it was entirely the same group of people, just now eating disco fries.

When I wasn't in the clubs or getting ready to go to the clubs, I was hanging out on the piers with all of NYC's finest, most legendary queens. And that is where my greatest transformation happened: I became a gay man. I wanted Max and Cesar, everyone in my family, and all these kids along the river to know that, though I was white, a biological female, and hetero, I was one of them. And so I started acting and talking exactly like them. If you've never heard it (or have never seen the documentary *Paris Is Burning*—which, child, why not?), then understand this: The pier queens spoke their own language, and it was the furthest thing from the Queen's English you could imagine.

Because Rosetta Stone doesn't offer a five-day immersion course in it, allow me to give you a quick lesson in Pier Queenese:

QUEEN'S ENGLISH: What I am about to tell you is the unabashed, 100 percent truth.
PIER QUEENESE: Here's the T, girl . . .

QUEEN'S ENGLISH: You look beautiful.
PIER QUEENESE: Oh, Miss Thing, you ah oh-vaaaaaah (which is derived from the word "over.")

QUEEN'S ENGLISH: I'm so happy.
PIER QUEENESE: Guurrrrl, I am liiiiiiiving.

QUEEN'S ENGLISH: Let me see your outfit.
PIER QUEENESE: Turn it, mama. Or, WEEEEERRRRRKKKKK! Past tense: She TURNT it OUT!

QUEEN'S ENGLISH: Definitely. No doubt, 100 percent.
PIER QUEENESE: Boots. The house down.

QUEEN'S ENGLISH: Ignore it.
PIER QUEENESE: Pay it dust.

QUEEN'S ENGLISH: She is feeling amazing and wants the world to know.

PIER QUEENESE: She is feeling her oats.

QUEEN'S ENGLISH: This is an amazing [insert any noun here].

PIER QUEENESE: Tens across the board.

QUEEN'S ENGLISH: OMG! Look at how gorgeous she is!

PIER QUEENESE: She betta werk!

QUEEN'S ENGLISH: Let's go tell a joke, be silly, and have a laugh.

PIER QUEENESE: Let's go have a kiki and carry on.

QUEEN'S ENGLISH: She was being dramatic and causing a ruckus.

PIER QUEENESE: She was CARRYING!!!

QUEEN'S ENGLISH: You are absolutely correct.

PIER QUEENESE: Okayyyyyy?

And that is exactly how I talked nearly twenty-four hours a day, seven days a week (except when I was at work or talking to my mother on the phone). Every other sentence out of my mouth sounded like a complete effing meltdown of a ball-walking category delivery. The deeper I got into the scene, the more abundant my Pier Queenese got. I opened my mouth and rainbow, glitter, and unicorns holding pink purses flew out. But understand something: I wasn't trying to fake the funk, I was being authentic . . . or so I thought.

THE TWE ALL SO DESPERATELY WANT TO BE ACCEPTED, which is why it's so easy, when you join a group (whether it's a new circle of friends, an office, or a community) to let it swallow you up. But I'm telling you now: Do not let that happen to you. Don't be so quick to give up your own identity just to fit in. Because, in the long run, just belonging to a scene isn't enough. To be a diva, you've got to cultivate your own strengths and your own personality within it. Hang on to what sets you apart, because that is what makes you special. When I look at all of my friends who survived those many nights on the piers, the ones who made it, the ones who are truly happy now, they are also the ones who never lost themselves there. They could pop, dip, and spin with the best of them, but they also studied dance, music, photography, fashion, or whatever was their personal passion. Sure, they no longer rule the piers . . . because now they rule the world.

One night, when we were on the pier, Vogueing, kikiing, and carrying on, Max, the gentlest and apparently the wisest of my circle, pulled me aside. "Guuurl, I'm worried about you," he said. "We love you very much. You're one of us. You're already in our family, so please do yourself a huge favor and stop acting like a faggot." To this day, I absolutely despise that *F* word, but I knew EXACTLY what he was trying to say. He went on, "Out of all of us, YOU have the biggest chance at a future. YOU are going somewhere. You will not be down here Vogueing on the piers forever, because you have talent. You don't have to be a gay man. You're already fabulous, so just be yourself."

Max was right. I had changed. So, I toned it down a bit. Instead of saying, "Guurrrlll, you ah oh-vaaaaaaah," I'd say, "Girl, you are ovah," and I'd top off that compliment with my own signature look of approval. It was my first step in realizing that my words had more power when I was saying them. Don't get me wrong: I'm not saying I stopped hanging out with my pier queens (as IF!) or loving my gays (that will never stop). I just realized I didn't have to give up my identity to be a part of the group. And you know what? When I revealed my even truer self to them, they loved me even more, and we got closer as a family. That's why to this day when I see baby gays jumping over hoops for attention or sheblamming themselves into the ER, my heart goes out to them, and I just want to hug them and tell them they don't have to try so hard. It'll be OK. And it will be.

RULE _no._ 8:

KEEP YOUR SHIT TOGETHER.

If you think for one minute that anybody you send a résumé to isn't going to Google you, check your Facebook, read your Twitter, watch your YouTube, and basically search for photos of you falling down drunk, then I've got some swampland in Florida with your name on it. I guarantee you this: They will find whatever is out there, and if what they discover does not make you look good, you'll miss out on big opportunities in your life, no matter how hardworking, enthusiastic, or otherwise smart you are. Don't get me wrong: I'm not saying you have to become a Mormon. I'm not going to judge you if you do a little partying. But what I am saying is this: If you're going to be a drunken fool, get ready for what's to follow. If you're going to let your boobs hang out, be prepared for someone else to post a photo of them swinging in the wind. Nobody else is going to look out for your best interests. That's your job, and if you don't take it seriously, that one moment of stupidity could haunt you for years.

That's why the one (and only) sex tape I made—with my husband, mind you—is under lock and key in a safe and will remain there until I am long gone and my children figure out the combination to the safe (that will be a fun posthumous viewing party!). It's also why I don't drink. The six times in my life that I have been drunk, I became someone I didn't like at all. Let me say this: I am a Virgo, and I admittedly have control issues. I was the girl who didn't know how drunk she was until she was crouched between two parked cars, puking on her own Doc Martens. And after I'd spew my Malibu and pineapple juice, my Kahlua and cream, my black Sambuca, basically anything with a sugar content of 5,000 grams or more, girl, that's when the party really started. Booze does things to me that make me want to do things to other people. It makes me lose all control of my sexual urges, like ZERO boundaries. If I'm Princess Sluttypants when I'm sober, give me a few cocktails and I'm suddenly Whorella, Queen of the Harlots. Every single one of those six times I got wasted, I'd throw myself at whichever guy or girl was within reach. Once in Manhattan, once in Brooklyn, and once in Jersey, I've even awakened in an orgiastic pit of naked people only to regret what I didn't even know. Not really my scene. And I'm damn lucky all of this happened before smartphones and the Internet. So, yeah, it didn't take long for me to realize drinking was not a good look for me. At all. Ever. I do, however, enjoy always being the sober one and watching the shenanigans. There is definitely a reason why the stuff is called "spirits."

Luckily, drugs never held much appeal for me either. I've smoked pot three times, twice in high school and once in college, and after the third time, I ate a dozen Boston cream donuts all by myself, which was not a path I wanted to go down. I did speed once too. I bought something called a Black Beauty from a girl named Susan in the bathroom of my high school, right before I sat down to take the SATs. I was so amped during the four-hour-long exam that rather than filling in the dots that correspond to the correct answers, I drew butterflies all over my answer sheet, which, of course, tanked my score and saddled me with six months of tutoring before my parents would let me take them again. That right there, all of the above is literally the full accounting of my drug and alcohol use. Ever.

But I lived and learned. And, by the time I moved to New York, my desire to become a star outweighed my desire to party. My priorities were clear (and so was my head), and that made a major difference in the trajectory of my life. We didn't have Facebook or Instagram in the late eighties, so we had to curate our images in real time. (No filters. No retakes. No Photoshop. No cropping out the ugly.) And for those of us like me, who didn't come from money or have connections, being seen in the flesh in the clubs was our only shot at landing a break. If we were ever going to get noticed by a celebrity, music producer, artist, fashion designer, or talent agent, it was going to happen there, and trust me, you didn't want them to see a sloppy, messy, falling-down girl who was trying to convince them she was the next Madonna.

Unfortunately, at any given time, about 90 percent of the kids in the clubs were too high out of their minds to notice. Dust, K, crack cocaine, meth—you name it, they were doing it (and often even being carted out on stretchers, only to return the very next night for an encore performance). So many of them had gobs of charisma, uniqueness, nerve, and talent, yet I watched them night after night miss their big breaks because they were too effed up to notice them when they came along.

Not me. Never me. I was often the only sober person among those fierce hordes of drunks and addicts, and I'm convinced that's part of the reason why I earned the attention of the legendary nightclub impresario Susanne Bartsch, the Swiss Miss of New York nightlife. (The other parts were, of course, because in my head I was sexy as hell and could out-Vogue any female who came for me, and most of the boys too.) Susanne was the most fabulous woman in the world, and she still is. She was a downtown boutique owner known for giving people such as John Galliano and Vivienne Westwood their starts in America, and her parties were what the *New York Times* would later call "the nightlife equivalent of a couture label." Everyone who was anyone in the music, fashion, and art worlds attended her events—Grace Jones, Thierry Mugler, Leigh Bowery, James St. James—and if you wanted to join the crowd, Kenny Kenny, Susanne's right-hand man, would have to choose you out of the eager masses waiting on the street. Not everybody got in. My baby, Kenny Kenny, would only tap-tap the most fabulous children, like those dressed in nothing but Swarovski crystals from head to toe, or in catsuits, or in designer labels, the tags of which they'd literally pull out to show off. ("Look, this is Mugler, baby.")

When Susanne approached me for the first time, I knew who she was. I mean, everyone knew who she was. I was on the dance floor at the Copa, Vogueing with my crew, when she leaned into my ear and, over the thumping bass, grunted in her thick German accent, "Doll, I love vat you do. I vant to pay you for it." She opened the door for me, and, baby, I strutted right through it in my six-inch stilettos. From that night on, I Vogued at all of her parties, just as I'd done in the clubs and in the balls on so many nights before—only now, I was getting paid for it. For $300 a night, I'd get up onstage and serve body-ody-ody. I'd wear a bra, hot pants, and boots, and I'd snatch my long blond ponytail so high and so tight my eyebrows were on the back of my neck. Even though I'd be a glistening fool (divas don't sweat, darlings, we glisten), I'd kill it all night long. I always brought my crew too. Out of my $300 take for the night, I'd pay Cesar, Jerome, Fidel, and Princess $50 each, plus free drink tickets. To be honest, these children cared waaaay more about the drink tickets than the cab fare home. Together, we worked all over town at Bentley's, the Red Parrot, El Morocco, the Tunnel, the Copacabana, and also at the first Love Ball, in 1989, an AIDS fundraiser attended by everyone from Carolina Herrera to Keith Haring to Madonna.

Because I kept my shit together, I was also able to notice the man who would eventually become one of the most important people in my life: RuPaul. And how could I not. He was a seven-foot-tall queen with an afro, dressed in a miniskirt, crazy earrings, and hooker heels. He'd dance through the audience, always smiling, always laughing. I was so enamored with Ru that I'd watch him all night long, as if we were the only two in the club. The joint could've burned down around us, and all I'd do was just stare at

THE

YOU SPEND HOURS PERFECTING THAT #SELFIE and hundreds, sometimes thousands on those clothes. So, when the time comes for you to walk the runway of life, don't be so effed up you stumble. It's not that the fabulous don't ever fall. (When we do, we do it spectacularly.) It's that if you're going to fall flat on your face, you want it to be because you reached for the stars and missed, not because you reached for that tenth drink and got pissed. Keep it classy, kids. Remember there is a time and a place for everything. Use your head.

him. He had this aura about him, and thank God, I was clearheaded enough to zone in on it.

If you're paying attention, you can learn so much from watching people, and that's all I'd do all night long from the main stage. It's where I got my real education. It's where I learned how to read—and own—a room. It's where I learned about star power, darling. And it's where I learned the simplest, but perhaps most important, lesson of all: If you want to succeed, the first thing you've got to do—before everything else—is just show the hell up (mentally and physically) fully prepared to take on whatever may be required of you. I know that Susanne would never have hired me if I'd been too drunk to dance, and if I'd missed that opportunity—who knows?—I shudder to think that I might never have met Ru. And when I look at who among my friends from that time made it, it's not the ones with only talent and ambition. We were all talented. We all wanted more for ourselves. It's the ones who simply kept their shit together enough to notice when they got noticed.

RULE _no._ 9:

BE THE HONEY _and_ WAIT FOR THE BEES.

To get to the top, you're going to need people around you who support not only your career but also your soul. And I'm not necessarily talking about your friends here. (Of course, they're important too. I personally keep a very tight inner circle, or so my husband raves.) No, I'm talking about the other _F_ word: "fans." You need them, now and always. Whether you're a receptionist or a CEO, the more fans you have surrounding you, the easier success will come to you (and keep coming to you) in every area of your life. The difference between divas and everyone else is that divas consider every person around them potential members of their adoration society. So, as a diva, know that when you're working in your office, dancing in a club, buying a book (ahem), shopping for new clothes, or making an upside-down half-caf skinny 108-degree latte, you have just one job: Win over everyone around you.

Luckily, we're all born with charisma. Some of us, however, just know how to channel that charm a little bit better than others, and as a result, fans are just drawn to them like pigs to . . . you get the point. Perfect example: Adore Delano. I say this with nothing but pure love, respect, and adoration, but you and I both know she was a not-quite-ready-for-primetime drag queen who wore messy-ass shake-and-go wigs and midcalf gowns. (Oh yes, honey, I am still talking about her hemlines.) I'm not being shady here. I'm just telling it like it is . . . or hopefully (fingers crossed) was. And yet despite her unpolished aesthetic, Adore is so incredibly charismatic, nothing else mattered in the end. I fell madly and truly in love with her, and she won lifelong, devoted fans—myself included—from the moment she uttered her first "Party!" That's magnetism, baby. If you're funny and you can carry on a conversation worth listening to, make it be known. If you've got it, werk it! And if you don't, go get an effin' candy dish, fill it with chocolate, and offer everyone you meet a piece. I'm dead serious.

I'm not saying I ever needed to bribe people to hang out with me. People have always been drawn to me from my earliest days. I am just saying that serving up some real sweetness, coupled with sweet realness, has definitely helped me in my life.

After I graduated from college at nineteen, I needed a job. My parents had taken a second mortgage out on their house to pay for my tuition, and room and board, and the moment I sissied my walk across that stage to get my degree, my mom said, "Congratulations. Sally Mae wants her money back." She wasn't messing around either. She literally handed me the book of payment slips, and from that day forward, I was responsible for paying not only my own living expenses but also my college loans.

I registered with a temp agency and almost immediately got permanently placed as a receptionist at a clothing showroom in NYC's famed Garment District called Casablanca and Fundamental Things. My main job was to answer the phone, and you know I worked that line like a diva. In my head I was Lily Tomlin's Ernestine the operator (Google it, young'ns). "Casablanca and Fundamental Thiiiiiings," I'd sing in my most sultry voice. It was all I could do to make that place seem more fabulous that it was. Everyone who worked there would have rather been working for Thierry Mugler, Oscar de la Renta, or Vera Wang, but instead they were stuck selling mid-price-point polyester clothing to Bible-toting Midwestern women. The customers weren't buyers from Bloomingdale's or Bergdorf's. They were the buyers from Dillard's and Bon-Ton.

You couldn't work at Casablanca and Fundamental Things and be a fashion snob, but the head bitch in charge certainly tried. She was this uptight woman named Gail who always wore full makeup, pumps, and a pencil skirt, and had her hair done up in a "Jersey poof" updo so shellacked it looked like a croissant in the back, helmet in the front. A "crullet," it you will. Though I lived for that, it was obvious that her main problem was that she clearly needed to get laid, and my main problem was that I needed to be able to sneak out for auditions whenever I had one. You already know this about me, but I do not stop until I get what I want. And Gail wasn't going to be the first one to take me down. Child, puh-lease. So here's what I did: On my lunch break, I went to the dollar store and hauled back a giant bag of candy, which I then set out in a dish on the edge of my desk. I also casually placed my pack of Marlboro Light 100s in plain view, a sign they were available for bumming. Finally, I stashed all the menus of the local restaurants in my top drawer, so if anyone ever got hungry, they'd come to me to place their order. Very quickly, my desk became the social center of the office. Everyone would stop by to grab some candy, have a smoke, order lunch, or just chat, and as a result, not only did I have more fun at work, but I also became more than just the receptionist. Prior to talking to me, all of the ladies at Casablanca and Fundamental Things saw me as a nineteen-year-old kid who fell somewhere between a mindless theater-college graduate with zero ambition and a gold-digging hooker looking for a sugar daddy. But after talking to me, they started to get to really know me and understand how serious I was about becoming a recording artist/ Broadway star. Pretty soon, some of them were even offering to cover the phones for me if I had an important audition. I eventually won Gail over too. Seeing how many fans I had in the office, she never made my absences an issue, and before long, she even started asking after my auditions and rooting for my success. Even the owner, Sam, was into my success! I would answer the phones, and when he would call, the first thing he'd ask was how my latest auditions were going. When I landed Seduction later that year, they were so happy they threw me a little going-away dinner when I had to quit the job to pursue my dream. It had been a tough start at a new job with a close-knit group of ladies

THE **T**CHILDREN, WINNING FANS, ONE BY ONE BY ONE, IS HOW YOU GET SHIT DONE.** And I'm not talking about using people either. I'm talking about forming real relationships. To win fans, all you have to do is just spread love (and, if necessary, also candy, cigarettes, and pastrami on rye). If you can make everyone within twenty feet of you genuinely feel better about themselves, or even just their day, by being around you, or simply just listening, you'll have not only loyal fans but also loyal friends. And when an opportunity does come along, they're the people who'll help lift you up so you can reach out and grab it. Remember this: somebody is always going to win the prize, so honey, why shouldn't it be you?

who had been working there for many years and had zero interest in widening their circle of friends. They all ended up being incredibly personable (even Gail) and likable when they took the time to talk to me. Who cares if I had to lure them at first with my candy and ciggy-butts bait? I am the honey, they are the bees, and in the end, they couldn't stay away from my desk. #Winning.

RULE _no._ 10:

CELEBRATE YOUR COMPETITION.

When you're out there fighting tooth and acrylic nails for success, you've got to get to know your competition. And I don't just mean the bitches to your left and right. I mean, _everyone_: the success-hungry masses nipping at your six-inch stilettos, and the one gorgeous diva who is already on top, who is already winning at everything you so desperately want to do. Study each of them— up, down, and sideways—like it's your job. Make it your mission to learn what they do well, and then start doing your own version of the same damn thing—only better.

Madonna has always been my idol from the moment she released her debut album, _Madonna_, in the summer of 1983. I was fourteen years old, and when I heard her for the first time, I would've sworn to you right then and there that the world had stopped spinning. Forget Belinda Carlisle. Madonna was who I wanted to be. And then—then!—two years later, she went and married my ultimate dream guy, Sean Penn, whom I'd been fantasizing about since _Bad Boys_ and then, of course, _Fast Times_ *at Ridgemont High*. Madonna was living the life I was meant to live, and I became obsessed with everything about her.

She was everything to me then, and she still is everything to me to this day. I love, adore, and respect her so much. In fact, I still have a huge *Truth or Dare* poster, which has survived my many cross-country moves, hanging on my living room wall. And in my office I have a sign that asks, "What would Madonna do?" Whenever I find myself stuck, or lost, or at a crossroads, it's the one question that shows me the way to the right answer every time. She is the true north on my diva compass, shining her superstar light on my path forward. Too much? Nah, I don't even think so.

OK, OK, children, she may have gotten a little loopy lately, and those grills were a bit much even for me, but you should never, ever forget what a trailblazer Madonna was. She always stood up for what she believed in, even if her beliefs weren't popular at the time. She was always an open and fierce advocate for the gay community, even when Elton John was still in the closet. She always embraced her sexuality and was never afraid to express it, even when the entire Catholic Church came down on her for it. (The Vatican once proclaimed one of her concerts one of the "most satanic shows in the history of humanity." Apparently, John Paul II was as big of a drama queen as Madge herself.) And she always had the power to surprise, delight, entertain, and even shock us, changing her image every time we saw her. Before the dawn of social media, I remember waiting with bated breath for her next video, her next magazine cover, her next tour, just to see

Seduction in motion.

Photoshoot with Seduction in Tokyo.

Sinoa and I always had fun when we were in Seduction.

Seduction performed in a mall and afterward was insanity! Security had to shut it down.

This was always the easiest place for
me to hold a mic.

This was the performance that changed everything for Seduction. It was for a radio station in Philly called Q102. They loved us so much they brought us back up to perform the same number because it was all we had!

At my birthday celebration at Mom's house. I had a Pekingese infatuation. I had four at one time; this one was Isis.

Working at Goldfingers gentlemen's club was one of the best experiences of my life. I had the cowboy hat on and the cigarette. I quit smoking when I was twenty-six.

Remember to never *ever* take yourself too seriously.

Not impressed on stage with S.O.U.L. S.Y.S.T.E.M.

Meeting my biological father, Wiss, for the first time.

Meeting my biological mother, Joanne, for the first time.

My biological family: (left to right) my baby sister Kim, sister Lisa, me, mother Joanne, and grandmother Irene.

The true loves of my life for now and forever; Marty and Arlene.

what amazing new look she'd unveil. And she never disappointed.

By the time I'd moved to New York City, my dream was clear: I wanted to become the next Madonna, and nothing was going to stand in my way, not even the queen herself. When I was twenty, just a month or so before I landed Seduction, the famous nightclub impresario Susanne Bartsch, who had already recruited me to Vogue at her downtown parties every week, invited me and my crew to Vogue on center stage for her first Love Ball, a star-studded event to raise awareness and money to fight AIDS. It was so crowded that you could hardly move, but everyone who was anyone was there: designers Carolina Herrera, Donna Karan, and Thierry Mugler; David Byrne of the Talking Heads; artist Keith Haring; *Vogue*'s Andre Leon Talley; RuPaul; Studio 54 owner Steve Rubell; gossip columnist Michael Musto. The *New York Times* wrote about the event, saying, "The Love Ball was to the typical charity affair what the Sex Pistols were to Mozart."

The evening had all the elements that make New York City nightlife remarkable: beauty, pageantry, celebrity, and gender confusion. Leading figures from the fashion industry were on hand to sponsor, perform, or judge in perhaps the biggest public display to date of "Vogueing."

I certainly wasn't the only one Vogueing that night. There were amateurs, giving it a go for charity, but I, of course, was not. I was the pro, brought in by Susanne to show how it's really done, and I was without a doubt serving up so much sexiness in the Roseland Ballroom that night that no one could've missed me. I wore my platinum-blond ponytail snatched high and tight, along with my

THE **WHEN COMPETITION GETS FIERCE,** as it always has and always will on the great dance floor of life, it's easy to get down on the other bitches gunning for you. It's easy to hate them for stealing your moves or for making you feel scared or for even existing. How dare they! But rather than throw shade and hate, here's what I want you to do instead: Fill your heart with gratitude and thank every single one of them for making you try harder, risk more, and be better than you ever would have been without them. Without the people who are constantly trying to outshine us, we would be the big, giant *C* word: complacent! (What did you think I was gonna say?)

usual bra, leggings, and boots. This time, I also added a new accessory: knee pads.

Legend has it (and Susanne Bartsch confirms it) that my idol, Madonna, was in the audience that night, and the Love Ball is where she was introduced to Vogueing for the first time. Of the event, which raised $400,000 to fight AIDS, Susanne has been known to brag, "Madonna came, and the next thing you know, there's the 'Vogue' video."

She's right, too. Ten months after the Love Ball, Madonna released "Vogue," and when I saw the video for the first time, I was absolutely gutted. Everyone in my inner circle, including Willi Ninja and Cesar Valentino, called me up, all, "Girl! That hair, that bra, those moves, your *everything*." And she picked Jose and Luis Xtravaganza, two the best Voguers on the scene and my shade-throwing rivals, to be her teachers and backup dancers. Once they teamed up, Madonna started doing everything I'd already been doing for the previous four years in the clubs. To say she was actually doing me might be presumptuous, but the coincidences were beyond.

Of course, in the short time between the Love Ball and "Vogue," my life had changed drastically. I'd landed Seduction and was touring the country and even shooting music videos. Michael Bay, who'd go on to direct *Armageddon, Pearl Harbor,* and all the gajillion *Transformers* movies, directed our music video for "Heartbeat" in Los Angeles. He's a great guy, and I got along famously with him. But, man, he is completely obsessed with tits! It was a tiny problem for me, literally, because believe it or not, at the time, I had *none*!

We're talking practically lowercase A-cups here. But Michael kept saying, "Could you push your boobs up more? Higher? More? Any more?" By the time we were actually filming, I was wearing two of the thickest padded pushup bras I could find, stuffed with my finest Lady Footlocker socks, and hoisted up to my chin. (If you watch that video on YouTube, you'll see me and my very obviously padded bra dancing in silhouette.)

After my video aired on MTV and the song hit #13 on the Billboard charts, Marthe, our label rep at Vendetta, called me up and said, "I want you to know something and I don't want you to get upset." Never a great a way to start a conversation. It turns out that that Madonna's people had called my people and accused them of promoting an artist—me!—who was too closely emulating Madonna, and Madonna was not happy with it. Oh, the SHADE!

Initially, I was devastated. But then it dawned on me. Madonna knows my name. She knows who I am. She knows I exist. And that gave me life. And, after that, the room kind of faded, and Marthe kept talking about something else and blah-blah this and blah-blah that, while I imaged Madonna's gorgeous lips repeating "Mii-chellle Vii-sage" slowly, over and over. I just thanked my lucky stars for shining on me, uh, wherever I am. At that moment, I realized I was fierce enough to make Madonna notice me. And that meant I was doing it right.

RULE _no._ 11:

BELIEVE YOU'RE THE BEST (_or_ FAKE IT UNTIL YOU ARE).

If you never struggle with self-doubt, then congratulations: You're perfect . . . and annoying. We get it. Now, die, robot, die! If you _do_ struggle with self-doubt from time to time (or, you know, even all the time), then welcome to the club—you're officially human. Do not let that nasty little voice in your head take over your life, or you could lose everything. I'm not being dramatic when I say that either. We all have this idea that if you have a down day, that's OK, because tomorrow you can start over again. New day, new you, and all that. And while that sounds nice, I think it's total bullshit. Insecurity is a greedy bitch, and she only stops when there's nothing left of you to take. So if you give in to her, even just a little, you will spiral downward, and the lower you feel, the harder it'll be to rescue yourself.

Never give up. Never surrender. Today is the day. What are we waiting for? We will be invincible. I love you, Pat Benatar.

OK, I'm going to let you in on a little secret that only Ru and my husband know: My confidence is a total act. Behind all of this hair and these incredible God-given cheekbones, I'm an insecure mess. Always have been. My inner saboteur, if I let her loose, tells me, "You're aging. You're overweight. You're washed-up. You're not worthy of anything. Not love. Not friendship. Not success. And most certainly not natural breasts." Right before a gig is when I'm always at my most vulnerable. My inner saboteur always sneaks up on me in my dressing room and grabs me by the (false) lashes, whether I'm taking my seat next to Ru at the judges' table on *Drag Race* or taking the main stage when I'm touring the world. But—and this is a huge "but," just like I like 'em—during the split second when I go from offstage to onstage, right as I'm about to sashay into the spotlight, I somehow find the courage, or maybe just the grit, to beat that nasty bitch back until I can no longer hear her voice over my own. Being able to find your fierceness, even in your weakest, most vulnerable moments, is what makes you a diva. Never—you hear me?—neeeeh-verrrrr let anyone see you sweat. I know that's a deodorant commercial, but it's a damn good one. And the reason you remember it is because it's true. (Sidebar: Dry Idea execs, call me. Let's tawk.)

My confidence, not my competence, earned me my big break when I was nineteen. I was sitting at the front desk, manning the phones of Casablanca and Fundamental Things, when my best friend at the time, Idalis, called. She was this stunningly gorgeous, twenty-six-year-old model and bartender at the Palladium. She was my style icon and, when we went out to the hip-hop clubs, my wing woman. (I couldn't get laid at the gay clubs, so I went to the hip-hop clubs when I needed to meet some meat that wasn't tucked.) Anyway, by the time I got out "And Fundamental Thiiiiiings" on the phone that day, Idalis interrupted me. "Hey, girl, listen to this! I just got into a girl group!"

"What?" I said.

"This guy was at the club and thought I was pretty and asked if I could sing, so I did!"

"What?!" I said.

Idalis filled me in on the group. Two producers, Robert Clivillés and David Cole, who you might also know as C&C Music Factory, were putting an act together quickly. They'd written a song called, "You're My One and Only (True Love)," and had the great Martha Wash ghost-record the vocals under the group-to-be's name, Seduction. (If you can't remember this song, I will sing you a line of the chorus, and you will never be able to forget it again. Even if you want to.) Vendetta Records, a subsidiary of A&M, signed this nonentity known as Seduction, and when the song started to climb the charts, venues all over the world were suddenly asking to book a group that never really existed. So, David and Robert became desperate to throw together a group, and to make a splash, they wanted it to be the first interracial girl group in music history. Idalis, by the way, is a Puerto Rican goddess.

"Do they have a white girl yet?" I asked. "Give me their number!" Idalis said yes, they did have a white girl already, and no, I couldn't have their number. She told me she didn't want to overstep or make them mad at her before she even started. "Idalis, I'm not going to embarrass you!" I said. "Give me their number!"

Eventually, she relented, and the moment I hung up with her, I dialed the digits she gave me. This was the first time in my life I literally had a direct line to someone in the music business. I was so friggin' nervous. This was really happening, and I was not gonna let the moment pass without giving it all I had to give. While the phone rang, I swallowed all of my self-doubt and

THE

IF YOU EVER FEEL YOURSELF GIVING IN TO YOUR INNER EVIL TWIN, KNOW THIS: In every battle, from lip-syncing to real life, presence always trumps perfection. Confidence trumps competence, so wear it like an accessory. Make it the last thing you put on before you leave the house every morning. It's taken me four long, sometimes tear-filled decades to learn that lesson. You know now that I don't believe in regret. I like to drive my life forward and try not to look in the rearview mirror, because what's done is done and nothing can change it. But if I could go back and talk to my nineteen-year-old self, I'd say, "Less hair bleach, more black eyeliner, and waaaay longer nails . . . but, most important, stop being so hard on yourself." One of my all-time favorite RuPaul quotes sums it up: "What other people think of you is none of your damn business." Life is hard enough already, and the only way to make it easier is to start loving yourself. And until you can do that, then, girl: You gotta fake it 'til you make it!

prepared a little speech for when someone, anyone, answered. Their manager picked up the phone. Without waiting for him to hang up on me, I said, "My name [pause for effect] is Michelle Visage. I hear you're putting together an interracial girl group and you need a white girl for it." When he told me, "Sorry, they already have a white girl," I countered, "Well they don't have me." I had nothing to lose, and honestly, I think he was just so impressed, or at least intrigued, by my confidence that he felt he needed to meet the crazy bitch on the other end of the line. Luckily, he couldn't see my hand shaking.

That night after work, I took off my big, bulky, fashion-savvy, cable-knit long sweater and walked fifteen blocks downtown to their office on Twenty-third Street in my Doc Marten boots, tight leggings, and even tighter cami. Their space looked nothing like I'd imagined Clive Davis or Tommy Mottola's would've looked. It was a small, plain office that appeared to be more suited to Dunder Miflin than a music-management company. But before I had any time to take it in, they buzzed me into this tiny little conference room with a tiny little conference table. I threw my shoulders back, dumped my bag on the floor, and said, "Hi-yeeee! I'm here to sing for you." And that's exactly what I did. I sang Teena Marie's "Déjà Vu," and though they seemed as captivated by me as one could be sitting under fluorescent lights at a conference table, they asked for another song. I gave them "I am Love" by Jennifer Holliday, who, if you don't know her, was—no exaggeration—a four hundred-pound, Tony Award–winning black gospel singer. Before I had to muster up the confidence to actually hit the high note, I conveniently stopped at that point in the song and was like, "Well?" Then David Cole said, "Why did you stop?" I said, "Do you need more?" and David retaliated with, "If you hit this note, you're in." I did, and they said, "Pack your panties. You're going to Virginia Beach."

Within a week, Idalis and I, along with our official black girl, April Harris, made our debut as Seduction at a club in Virginia Beach, opening for Buster Poindexter. (I'd insert a joke here, but I think opening for Buster Poindexter is punch line enough.) Six weeks later we recorded an entire album, *Nothing Matters Without Love*, and in under a year, we had sold more than half a million copies of it. And all of this happened because I refused to give in to my self-doubt. I refused to believe anyone on the entire planet might possibly do a better job as the white girl in Seduction than I could, including, by the way, the poor girl who had already landed the gig until I came along. Look, I know I'm not the best singer in the world (I have a pretty voice; I'm just no Mariah or Xtina), and if I listen to my inner voice, I could probably even convince myself that I sound more like Roseanne. But I've learned that real divas are born in those darkest, most private moments, when your inner saboteur is trying to shout you down. That's when your true strength and grit will be tested. It won't happen when all eyes are on you. It'll happen when you're staring at yourself in the mirror before you leave your house, or your dressing room, or your car. That's the moment when you choose to burn out or shine bright. That's when you decide to fall to the negativity or rise to superstardom no matter the circumstance.

RULE _no._ 12:

EXPOSURE ISN'T MONEY, *but* SOMETIMES IT CAN BE WORTH MORE.

If you are trying to break into the music, fashion, film, TV, or any other kind of media-based business, I guarantee you that at some point in your career, especially if you're just starting out (and maybe even if you're not), someone somewhere will ask you to do work for them for free, though they won't actually say the word "free," because that would be totally presumptuous of them and insulting to you. Instead, they'll say something like, "We can't actually pay you, but we can offer you great exposure!"

You and I both know your work is worth something, so part of me wants to tell you to put your hand on your hip, swivel your neck, and answer, "Bitch? Puh-lease." Because, when it comes down to it, exposure won't put food on your table. You can't explain to your credit card collectors that you have no money but lots and lots of people know who you are. Your elevated Klout Score can't keep your car running or your lights on. You literally cannot bank on exposure. But—and you knew that was coming, didn't you?—if you get the right kind of exposure, you can trade that shit in one day. Big-time.

When I landed in the girl group Seduction, I thought I was on my way. "Watch out, world. Visage has arrived!" My queens back in the clubs were giddy for me. My parents were bursting with pride. Even my middle-aged lady coworkers at Casablanca and Fundamental Thiiiings toasted me with cheap champagne at our office party, served in paper cups.

But there was just one catch: Before we could go on tour or record our album, David Cole and Robert Clivillés, the musical geniuses behind Seduction, presented me, Idalis, and our third, April Harris, with a contract that they required us to sign, seal, and deliver. So, not wanting to risk losing out on my dream and believing their assurances that I was indeed going to be a rich and famous pop star one day, I put my trust in them, signed on the dotted line, and hoped for the best.

Signing that contract was probably one of the biggest mistakes of my life, but like everything, it was a learning experience, and I wouldn't trade those memories for anything. I didn't, however, realize just how bad it was until recently . . .

Unbeknownst to me, I basically sold my twenty-year-old soul to two savvy music producers. Under the contract I signed, the producers paid Idalis, April, and me almost nothing but seemingly pocketed almost every remaining penny that our group earned. Thus, no matter how many albums we sold or concert seats we filled, Idalis, April, and I were paid a flat, piddly weekly salary. It was just more than double what I was making as a nine-to-five receptionist at a midtown purveyor of polyesters. To put that in perspective, this was one of the worst deals in music history, on par with that of TLC's and the Supremes'.

In the beginning, I just had stars in my eyes. For our first gig, which was just a few days after my audition, Robert and David handed April, Idalis, and me some cash and sent us out to shop for our own wardrobe. We went to New York's Eighth Street, which at the time was The End for fashion, and with our tiny allowance we had just enough for three matching half shirts and three pairs of billowing ankle pants. I was the group's mouth, and coincidentally the Virgo, so I took charge and volunteered to be the wardrobe girl. I was responsible for the costumes when we flew to Virginia Beach for our first show and opening for the pompadoured Buster Poindexter, who was best known for his rendition of "Hot, Hot, Hot."

For that gig, they put us up at the Holiday Inn Express, all three of us in one tiny room, and when I opened my suitcase to get ready for the night, it seems I'd somehow forgotten April's outfit. It was a complete mistake and I felt horrendously guilty, so I offered to take her out and buy her another on my own credit card. Forget it. April just kept mad-dogging me. Gurl, it's not even human how mad she got at me. She immediately jumped to the conclusion that I was trying to sabotage her, and no matter what I did, she held tight to that ugly theory for as long as we worked together. Her hatred of me was palpable, and so we stayed as far as away from each other as possible, which wasn't always easy considering we shared not only the stage, but also hotel rooms and a tour bus. I may not have been earning much money, but I was learning how to manage difficult group dynamics, which has actually helped me later in my life.

After that gig, we returned to New York and set to learning our songs for our first album, *Nothing Matters Without Love*, which we released six weeks later. It was actually our only album, but of course we didn't know that at the time. Oddly enough, our biggest single, "Two to Make it Right," was my least-favorite song, and I was so happy it was assigned to April. Yup, that song was meant to be sung by just her, but the record company heard something big in the demo and decided to make it a duet by having me sing half of the lines. Oh, April loved that (sarcasm). The real T? I've always hated that song, and I still do. It's just so bubble gum and soulless. I was trying to be Teena Marie, not Marie Osmond. Even so, the song struck a chord with plenty of other people. Four months after we released the album, "Two to Make it Right," hit #1 on the *Billboard* Hot Dance Club chart; a month later, it reached #2 on the *Billboard* Hot 100; and by May, the album was certified gold. Why didn't it go to #1 if it was such a hit? We can thank Paula Abdul and that damn animated MC Scat Cat. A cartoon cat with an even more unfortunate name. "Opposites Attracted" them right to #1.

We worked our tight little asses off to sell that album, but no matter how much effort and hustle we put into it, Robert and David were seemingly the only ones making money, and we were none the wiser. To launch us, they sent us on a six-month radio tour and the deal was we'd travel from city to city and go on air, do an interview, and perform a few live songs, and in return the station would start spinning our record. As we watched our album move up the charts, we started to realize just how unfair this all was. Idalis, being a fiery Brooklyn-born-and-bred fighter, couldn't keep her anger under control. We were sisters, always as tight as could be, and we saw eye to eye on music, boys, fashion— everything except how to handle our emotions. She was so frustrated by our near servitude that eventually she just boiled over. She became resentful, and she'd do things like strut into a radio station, get in the DJ's face, and say, "Why the f*ck aren't you playing our record already? Everyone in the country is on it, why aren't YOU?" God, I loved her tenacity.

But alas, after the umpteenth episode like this, they pulled her aside to talk to her and tell her that she couldn't act that way, that it was accomplishing the exact opposite of what she was trying to do. After about six months, Robert and David fired her from the group. I begged them to give her another chance, but they wouldn't listen. Idalis wanted me to leave, too, in solidarity with her, and when I didn't—after all, this was still my dream, even though it was a broke-ass one—she felt betrayed and refused to talk to me for years. That broke my heart. I was devastated. Chalk that up to another lesson learned: I may not have been able to protect my own bottom line, but I was learning how to protect something even more valuable to me: my reputation.

By the summer of 1990, Seduction, which now consisted of me, April, and a new girl, Sinoa Loren, was on fire, and our label, A&M, sent us out on an eight-month-long tour through the U.S.,

Canada, and Japan with the hottest (both literally and figuratively) act at the time, Milli Vanilli. I finally felt official. We had a super-sweet tour bus that came with a supersweet driver named Boots, we had an actual choreographer and a stylist, and we finally got our own rooms whenever we stayed at a hotel. And yet, despite the fact that we were performing night after night, regularly selling out fourty thousand-seat arenas filled with screaming fans who knew all of the lyrics to all of our songs, I was still struggling to pay my most basic bills at home. Robert and David were home in New York, making money off of us hand over fist, and we were still only pulling a fixed paycheck of about a grand a week. But again, we were clueless. We thought that was the way it was.

I remember our first gig with Milli Vanilli. It was in Louisville, Kentucky. Motivated by equal parts courtesy and curiosity, Sinoa, April, and I went into the stadium to watch our tour mates' first sound check. And sure enough, "Girl, You Know It's True" was blasting, but the boys were nowhere in sight. That's when I had my first inclination that something might be up with them. I mean, in concert, Seduction sung to track too. Back then, every-body who did huge, full-on, choreographed concerts did—it was just the best way to do it so you didn't huff and puff on the mic and sound hideous when it was time for a vocal to come out of your mouth. It was pretty much the industry standard at the time, but, of course, we all sang our own albums, and if the track ever failed during a concert, which it did from time to time, we all could still sing live. When that happened, by the way, the audience would go wild. They loved it. Milli Vanilli, however, we'd later learn, couldn't sing a single note. In fact, these poor guys were just a couple of dancers from Munich who had been secretly hired as professional lip-syncers. They didn't sing at all on tour, but the real scandal was that they didn't sing on their album either.

After that strange sound check, we had a tour meeting that night, and that's where we got to meet the boys for the first time. I remember the moment exactly. Everyone on the tour—us, the roadies, the sound techs, our bus driver, Boots—was sitting on the floor in a hallway in a hotel. About an hour into our meeting the Vanilli boys walked in. I thought I'd be attracted to Rob Pilatus, the light-skinned one with the blue eyes, but he was so harsh that he quite honestly scared me. He was always mean and controlling. Onstage, he may have been hot, but in person, he was a total turnoff. Fabrice Morvan, however, was so sweet and warm and French and chocolate brown, and though his English was terrible, we had an instant connection—and a sizzling- hot love affair that began the first night we met and lasted throughout our entire tour.

At the time, they were both huge druggies. After each concert, we'd sit around on couches backstage, and someone would always show up with a silver platter. On it were long lines of powdery white cocaine, which they, along with plenty of the cast and crew, snorted like it was Pixy Stix. Though they would always politely offer some to me, I never took so much as a single bump, fearing not only for my life—I knew I'd be the one to try it and die on the spot—but also my career. I saw firsthand how unearned success can poison a person, and I vowed that I'd always work hard, so

I'd know deep down that whatever I got, I actually deserved. My mantra: I have further to go, further to go, further to go. I'm so proud of myself for always staying clean.

Everything—my relationships with Fabrice, Milli Vanilli, Seduction—fizzled out as quickly as it started. By the end of our tour, Milli Vanilli had been outed as frauds and their Grammy

THE

T DON'T BE AFRAID TO STAND UP FOR YOUR-SELF, PROTECT YOUR INTERESTS, AND FIGHT FOR WHAT'S FAIR. You deserve it. It's not rude to ask for a fair deal. It's smart. And if someone isn't offering you one, you have to decide in your heart whether the exposure is worth it to you. As a rule of thumb, I think generally if they're asking you to get naked, pose on a car, have sex, pee, or eat bugs on camera, the exposure will not be worth it, no matter how much they're paying you. None of that, I assure you, will build your career. But everything else might be worth your consideration and possibly, someday, even something more.

had been revoked. I was thoroughly disenchanted with Seduction and still as broke as ever, and we performed our last show as a group on New Year's Eve 1991, at a club called Stocks and Bonds in Boston. It was a fitting name for our final venue, since the issue of money, or the lack thereof, had been on our minds for more than a year. By this time, all the members of Seduction, past and present, were completely over it. April and I could hardly stand to share the stage anymore, and we were all just done with one another, personally and professionally.

I never got rich off of Seduction. In fact, I never got a dime from any of those songs. I never liked that business part of show business, and I still don't. But I can say with an honest heart that even though I was taken advantage of, in other ways I'm grateful for it. In what lifetime does a young girl from Jersey get to live out her dream like that? If I hadn't done it, I wouldn't have the experience of performing in front of gazillions of people. I wouldn't have learned how to work as part of a team, even when your team is losing and the members are fighting. I wouldn't have had the chance to see the entire country, plus Japan. I wouldn't have the patience I have today to deal with the queens whom I tour with for *Drag Race*, who think they're entitled to a private jet, a personal chef, and a suite at the Four Seasons—and complain when they don't get it.

RULE _no._ 13:

NEVER GIVE UP ON YOURSELF. NE-VER.

There will be a time in your life when you want something (or someone) so badly you think you might keel over and die if you don't get it. Then, like the badass you are, you steel your nerves and risk everything you've got to get it: your ego, your heart, your time, maybe even your money. Now, in the Lifetime made-for-TV movie version of your life, you'd totally triumph. There'd be a swell of music, a slow clap started by an enemy-turned-friend, and then happy tears all around. In real life? Sorry, baby, it just doesn't always work that way. Massive, messy, sloppy, heart-crushing, tear-inducing, soul-sapping failure is just a part of life, and if it isn't a part of yours, then you're either the luckiest doll on the face of the planet or you're doing something wrong. That is, if you never, ever fail, you're playing it way too safe. And safe is boring. Safe is stagnant. Safe leads to nothing but pure, unadulterated mediocrity, and divas are anything but mediocre. You've got to take risks. Big ones. That's how greatness happens. And if you f*ck up, well then, try again. And again. And again. And again. Failure is part of what will make you great.

In my life, I'm proud to say I've risked everything—and failed spectacularly. After Seduction broke up in the winter of 1991, I had nothing to my name but a bruised ego and pile of credit card debt. No savings, no investments, no royalties, no fairy godmother (or record label bigwig) opening doors for me, and basically no clear path forward. Everyone I knew—my family, my South Plainfield crew, my musical theater classmates, my gays, my Casablanca coworkers, Madonna Louise Ciccone—had watched me "make it," landing a record deal, filming music videos, and touring the country, and then less than two short years later, they all watched me fall as quickly as I'd risen. My lifelong dream of becoming a pop star was officially dead, and I had nowhere to turn. Or so I thought.

While I had no plan, luckily, I still did have friends, and one of my closest, let's call her Jennie (changing her name as her family has no clue she stripped), made it her personal mission to help me get back on my feet. She and I were living next door to each other in a four-unit townhouse complex in Belleville, New Jersey. Oh, the glamour! (Incidentally, the other two units in our complex were occupied by Angel "Love" Vasquez of the Latin freestyle group TKA, which featured me on its 1990 hit "Crash," and Roger of 2 In a Room—you know, the "Wiggle It" boys. If reality shows had existed back then, I'm sure we could've landed our own. We could've called it *Full Freestyle Townhouse*.)

Anyway, Jennie was a stripper at a seedy but well-known joint in Queens called Goldfingers, and she was earning in four nights as much as I had in an entire month with Seduction. So when she offered to make some introductions for me, I took her up on it without hesitation. Stripping seemed like my only option at the time. It was the only job that I was qualified to do that'd pay me that kind of cash, and dancing was something I knew I did really well. So why not shake my moneymaker and actually make some money?

Goldfingers was in a squat, black-and-tan building nestled between a Burger King and a car wash on Queens Boulevard in Rego Park, Queens, just across the East River. And when Jennie opened the door and nudged my ass inside, it was the first time in my life I'd ever stepped into a titty bar. The interior of this one was darker than I'd ever imagined—black walls, black tables, black chairs, black carpet, barely there lighting—and it was full of lonely businessmen in cheap suits, drinking even cheaper whiskey. They each sat around the foot of the stage, in the middle of any given afternoon, ogling these voluptuous but vacant girls, who were baring their big ones for their crumpled dollars.

By the time I set foot in the club on that snowy day and saw the girls swirling around those greasy poles, I'd changed my mind. I couldn't put myself out there like that. So instead, Jennie, who was always quick on her feet, told me that she had something else up her G-string. She had heard that the hot-oil wrestlers were in need of a new announcer because the current girl was pregnant and was starting to show, so she had to leave. Jennie then dragged me down into the basement of Goldfingers and introduced me to a guy named Phil, who ran the hot-oil wrestling. Phil was a chunky, obvious former steroid user who wore a bandana to hide his hair plugs and a girdle to hide his paunch. And as if you couldn't have guessed from that description, we hit it off right away. He needed an announcer, and I needed a job, and the moment he found out I was a former member of Seduction, he hired me for $500 in cash a week, plus whatever tips I'd earned.

So from that day on, six nights of the week, I'd make that hour-long drive to Queens (on a good night, leaving Jersey at three p.m. to avoid Lincoln Tunnel and Midtown Tunnel traffic) in my white '92 Nissan Pathfinder, and take my place in the basement outside of the boxing ring. We usually entertained a slew of drunken bachelors and horny twenty- to forty-year-old men two times a night—one show at nine p.m. and one at eleven p.m.—and it was my job to use my big mouth and cutting sense of humor to auction off a round in the ring with each sexy wrestler. Usually, I'd start the bidding at thirty dollars, but by the time I was finished coaxing the crowd, the girls would always go for between one and three hundred dollars (and the girls loved me for that). Once we had our highest bidder, the chosen wrestler would spray him down with oil and then shove her tits in his face and hump him in the ring until he couldn't take it anymore. Afterward, the wrestlers would then go into the audience and bounce on the other guys' laps (code word for "penis") for a dollar. I know it sounds crass, but this is the honest-to-God truth of what these poor girls literally did. No exaggeration. I had two jobs: Keep the crowd spending, and call out the creepers, who'd start fondling themselves pretty much out in the open, which was against the rules. On lucky nights, I'd walk the room for tips, and if I let the boys stuff them into my bra, I'd often collect an extra few crisp hundreds. I considered that quite a talent, as I was the only one fully clothed.

This. This, was my new life. No more arena shows, singing in front of sixty thousand screaming fans. No more cushy private tour buses. No more tricked out dressing rooms. No more music-video shoots. No more love affairs in fancy hotel rooms with a Grammy-award-winning pop star. Nope. Instead, I was working a cordless RadioShack mic for an audience of drunken bachelor-party boys in a claustrophobic strip club basement so moist you'd get herpes if you touched anything. I fell so fast I almost got black eyes from my own bozooms.

One day I'm a world-famous pop star. The next, I'm a sub-ground not quite- stripper, car commuting to the most soulless club in New York City's second most soulless borough—no offense, Queens.

You'd probably call this my rock bottom, and I totally see why. But you know what? I don't see it that way, because I never gave up on myself. I may have failed to become the pop star I'd dreamed of, but I was a survivor, and this was me surviving. I never saw my new gig at Goldfingers as something that was beneath me, because nothing was beneath me. Not then, not now. I was putting food on my table, and I was proud of that. I was taking care of business. I was doing what I had to do to get by, and I did it like a diva with my head held high. As the late great Maya Angelou once said, "You may not control all the events that happen to you, but you can decide not to be reduced by them." She's right. A diva will never allow herself to be reduced, no matter how shitty her circumstances get.

Besides, I was learning, and making friends. The hot-oil wrestlers at Goldfingers were to the strippers as drag queens are to beauty-pageant winners. While the strippers had their established routines and mindlessly went through the motions of what was expected of them (over and over and over again), the wrestlers were confident, campy, and full of personality. Picture the Village People in G-string bikinis and you've got a pretty good idea of my new coworkers. One would dress as a construction worker, another as a football player, another as a cop. And they welcomed me into their family with open, albeit greasy, fake-tanned arms. Together, we had a supportive, uncomplicated relationship, which was something I never had with Seduction. And these wrestlers were some of the strongest girls I've ever met. They taught me how to stay foxy and fierce no matter what, and they taught me how to find the fun in any situation. And most important, emceeing there taught me how to use my voice in a whole new way. I've held on to every single lesson I learned there to this day.

After about five months gigging in that disgusting Queens basement, Goldfingers opened a ritzy new club in Manhattan on 11th Avenue in Chelsea. It was the opposite of the Queens outpost: clean, bright, not at all seedy. They recruited me, along with a select few star wrestlers and strippers from Queens and a few new strippers bussed in from Houston, Texas, to open the club, and we catered to the celebrities who'd come by with their entourages every night. LL Cool J, who had recently released "Mama Said Knock You Out," was a regular. So were Axl Rose, Slash, and also my imaginary boyfriend, Sean Penn, who'd divorced Madonna a few years prior. His bodyguard actually approached me one night and said, "My client wants to meet you. He thinks you look like his ex-wife." By the way, worst pickup line in the history of the universe. I said, "Who is your client?" When he told me it was my dream man, I absolutely lost my shit. But rather than rip my clothes off and sit on his lap, which is what I really wanted to do, I played it super cool. "If he wants to talk to me," I said, "tell him to come here." He never did, and that was the end of my relationship with Sean Penn. (He couldn't have handled me anyway. Obviously.)

Anyway, I emceed at that strip club six nights a week for a year and a half straight, and eventually David Cole and Robert Clivillés had the nerve to approach me again with the grand promise of launching my solo career. Clive Davis, the founder of Arista Records, was a fan of mine, they said, and he wanted to meet with me right away. Of course I agreed to the meeting. Who wouldn't? I was getting a second shot at my dream, and this time, I was even hungrier for success.

Robert and David hired alleged backup singers for me

The headshot I used to audition for QVC. I still have no idea
why I didn't get the job with a headshot like this.

THE PEOPLE HANDLE DISAPPOINTMENT IN DIFFERENT WAYS. Some people get depressed. Others get angry. Others get self-destructive. But guess what? If you go out and get loaded night after night or if you curl up in bed with a half a gallon of Dreyer's French Silk ice cream and justify it because it's lower fat (what??), and give in to those voices that tell you you're a loser, or if you start acting like an asshole to everyone you meet, you're still going to have to face your failure the next morning. It's not going anywhere. And while it's nice to have friends and family to cry to in these dark moments, you cannot count on them to fix it for you. Only you can do that. You are stronger than you think, and now is the moment when you've got to dig deep and summon all the strength you've got.

So, if you f*ck up, if you humiliate yourself, if you try for something great and fall flat on your flawless face twice, here's what to do: First, take comfort in knowing that you're in great company, including mine. I guarantee you that every single diva you can think of has stumbled not just at some point in her life, but at many points in her life, and it's part of what makes them all so strong and so divine. The bigger the failure, the closer to greatness. Second, acknowledge just how incredibly shitty you feel, because you're going to feel really shitty for a while. Scream, punch a pillow, do what you need to do to get it out of your S.O.U.L.

S.Y.S.T.E.M.—I mean system—and then let it go as fast as you can. Do not hold on to those negative emotions for one millisecond longer than you have to, because all that negative energy will destroy your mind and your body. Third, figure out what went wrong so you don't repeat the same mistakes. That's what wisdom is all about. You've got to earn it to learn it. There's no other way. And last, take action and move on. I swear to you, things will get better, but only if you make them better. You can't expect your life to change without you doing the work it takes to change it. Don't just sit there and cry. You are not a victim. You're a diva. And don't wait either. Yesterday does not exist and tomorrow may never come, so it's up to you to figure out how to make your life better today. There is always something you can do at any given moment to spark the change you want to see, and it doesn't have to be big. If you're not happy at work, dust off your résumé. If you're not happy in your relationship, open your own bank account, and start putting away a few dollars at a time so you have the money to leave (SO important to have). If you're not happy with your weight, set aside a half hour to take a walk. I don't care what you do, as long as you do something. Your journey does not end with one stumble. Or two. Or three. Or a hundred. Divas never quit. Divas never give up. Divas always rise up, preferably on hydraulics with pyrotechnics shooting above an arena of adoring fans. But you know what? Sometimes just rising out of bed will do.

(remember, this was pitched as a solo gig)—the amazingly lovely and immensely talented Octavia Lambertis, Jamal Alicea, and Gary Michael-Wade—and though our vibe was a little too Michelle and the Pips for my taste, we all got along great. The only catch was, after a few rehearsals, David and Robert broke it to me that we'd be marketed not as Michelle Visage but as S.O.U.L. S.Y.S.T.E.M., featuring Michelle Visage. I was enraged. I remember arguing with them: "What? This was to be MY turn! My solo shot!" and "What's with all the stupid periods anyway? What the hell is it supposed to stand for?" But they didn't care, and eventually, realizing I had no other choice, I got over it.

After a few great gigs on the road, we went into the studio and recorded seven kick-ass songs, only one of which ever made it on air. "It's Gonna Be a Lovely Day" was featured on *The Bodyguard* soundtrack—Track 9, baby!—and, in 1992, it became one of the longest-running #1 hits on the *Billboard* Hot Dance Club play chart.

Unfortunately, when it came time to deliver the other tracks, including a duet with Mark Wahlberg, to Arista, they never delivered the album for reasons that are to this day still unknown to me. The thing is, the songs that I recorded were SO amazing, like waaay-before-their-time amazing, which kills me, since I know how much the world would've flipped over the tracks. As you can deduce, without an album, Arista dropped us faster than you can say "Ice Ice Baby." I watched my dream die again, and let me tell you, it doesn't really hurt any less the second time around.

RULE _no._ 14:

KEEP IT REAL, EXCEPT FOR YOUR TITS.

Girl, you know I'm a fan of facades. I love me some men dressed as women, women dressed as men, women dressed as men dressed as women (ahem), and everything in between. Just by playing with our appearance, we can express ourselves, change our own self-image, challenge society's rules, and, let's not forget, have a ton of genderf*cking fun. But here's the thing: You cannot live a lie and be happy. And to be one million percent clear, living a lie means you're not being completely, soul-baringly honest with yourself. Drag is not a lie to yourself, unless you're trying to be a pretty queen and pretty is not your thing, or you're trying to be a comedy queen and you can't even tell a knock-knock joke. A fake nose? Not a lie. Cheek implants? Not a lie. Fake tits? Please. Your truth lies in your heart and soul, not under your skirt or in your push-up bra.

Speaking of truths, I have to tell you a secret, so sit down and steady your pretty little self: The titties you see jacked up to my chin every Monday night on *Drag Race* did not come to me naturally. I bought my first pair when I was twenty-one and still in Seduction. I'd desperately wanted boobs since I was ten and saw my first *Playboy*, which was conveniently stashed under my dad's side of my parents' bed. I couldn't believe my eyes! As time went on I realized that Dad had a serious *Playboy* addiction. I went through each and every one of the hundreds of them stashed behind his workbench in the basement and dreamed of what my boobs would look like once I hit puberty.

By the time I turned fifteen, I still hadn't gotten my lady cycle and there was not a breast to be found. Yet I never gave up hope. Since my friend Susan had moved on to B-cups already, surely I wasn't far behind. Susan was stunningly gorgeous, model gorgeous, and she was as boob-obsessed as I was. In the eighth grade, she and I chipped in whatever allowance money we had and secretly sent away for a breast-enlarging cream from the back of a magazine called *La Vive*. When it finally came, we rubbed that cream into our boobs daily after school and whammo! Not a thing happened for either one of us. Talk about a letdown. Susan grew older and her boobs grew larger, just as Mother Nature planned, but apparently Mother slept through her alarm the day she was to make me a "woman." She finally came to me when I turned sixteen, but she stayed in the basement. I literally never grew a breast larger than a training bra. Not even an A-cup, and for me that didn't work. All I ever wanted was a set of *Playboy* boobs, and instead I got *National Lampoon*. As you may remember, when I talked to my biological mom for the first time, my very first question was, "Why do I have no

THE DIVA RULES

boobs?" I'd had them on my mind until I literally had them on my mind, and my first set cost me eleven grand, which I put on my Visa card and never looked back. In my mind *this* was what credit cards were created for.

Anyway, I went to this fancy Upper East Side doctor, who had done my stripper friend Jennie's boobs, which were high and tight, and also Shirley Bassey's face-lift, which, gawd, was even higher and tighter. I told him I wanted my As turned into Ds, and after marking my chest with a Sharpie, he put me under, playing "Goldfinger," a nod to the name of Jennie's strip club (and later mine). You've gotta love a plastic surgeon with a sense of humor. Or, you know, not.

When I woke up and looked at my expensive new rack, I was so f*cking pissed off. "Irate" doesn't begin to describe the fury I felt. I wanted more than anything to have boobs like Pamela Anderson's, but rather than abide by my wishes, this asshole gave me 110cc saline implants. I paid eleven grand to become barely a B-cup. "Are you f*cking kidding me?" I yelled, looking in the mirror, still hazy under the anesthesia.

"Calm down," he said. "You're only ninety-eight pounds. You just don't have enough skin to stretch over anything larger."

"This is not what I wanted," I said, before breaking down into angry tears. "I never wanted to look natural. Natural is not my thing, nor does it interest me!"

Later, when Seduction broke up, I needed money to support myself, and I thought that stripping was the only way I could earn it. I also knew that no man without a magnifying glass was going to pay any cash to see my tiny silicone ta-tas, so I decided to make another investment in my future. A second boob job would cost me another five digits, but if I was as successful as Jennie, I figured I'd earn that back in literally just a couple of weeks at Goldfingers. So, like an asshole, I went back to the same doctor who'd given me my first set. I was basically just so shit-scared of anesthesia, and since I'd lived through my first surgery with him, I thought he was, if not the smartest choice, then at least perhaps the safest one. Right before I went under, I sat up on the operating table, my hair in one of those surgical poofs, and threatened him: "If I wake up and my tits are not the size of my head, you are going to pay the ultimate price." He laughed and told me to think happy thoughts. I dreamed of watermelons and halter tops.

When I eventually came to, I was so nauseated from the anesthesia that I could hardly focus. My mom was with me, and seeing the color, or lack thereof, in my face, she said, "This is it, Michelle. You're never doing this again." The doctor had given me a C-cup, one barely noticeable size up from the Bs he'd given me before, and when I saw them, I started crying and practically didn't stop until my chest was healed.

I was fully drained, emotionally and financially, which only made me more determined to nail my audition at Goldfingers. Jennie came with me, and as we made our way through the snarl of midtown traffic in my Pathfinder, I tried to mentally prepare myself to climb on that sweat-streaked stage and take all of my clothes off for any guy who'd give me a twenty. Or fiver. I'd already danced in clubs for years wearing next to nothing, and I once did a fashion show in a sheer top with no bra. Could stripping really be that much different?

In the car, as we were listening to "Pour Some Sugar on Me" by Def Leppard, Jennie started prepping me for the audition. John, the general manager of Goldfingers, would choose a song, and when it started playing, I was expected to hop onstage, take my clothes off, and dance, spin, twirl, and stick my tits and ass in his face, as if he were a paying customer.

"If you turn him on, he'll hire you," she said.

And right there, in the middle of the Queens Midtown Tunnel, is when I decided that I couldn't do it. I couldn't be a stripper, and not because I had any moral qualms about it. I have a shitload of respect for those women—single moms, most of them—for doing whatever they had to do to turn it out night after night to support themselves and their kids. But me? I knew I wouldn't be able to check out that way. I'm way too much of a clown to get on stage naked and gyrate to "Pour Some Sugar on Me" with a straight face, and I knew if that was what was expected of me, there was no way I would ever make a dime. Being a serious, sexy stripper was not my truth. This may surprise you, but my wits, not my tits, are my greatest strength.

You know how the rest of this story goes. When we got to Goldfingers, Jennie introduced me to the hot-oil wrestling guy instead, and since wagging my tongue came far more naturally to me than wagging my tail, I became an emcee rather than a stripper, which ultimately led me to my decades-long and successful career in radio.

My truth became crystal clear to me in the Queens–Midtown Tunnel. I had tried to convince myself I was someone else, someone who'd take her clothes off for cash, but in that dark under-the-river passageway, a light clicked on for me: I became even more

THE

T HAD I GOTTEN UP ON THAT STAGE AT GOLD-
FINGERS THAT DAY, I probably would've gotten the job, and maybe I would've even made bank doing it. But I know it would've cost me my soul, and even for a thousand dollars a night I could never have bought it back. Listen to your gut. Find and respect your own boundaries. Do what feels right to you, not what feels right to someone else. And always, always live your truth. That is the only way you'll ever be happy.

certain of who I was. I was going to use my voice, not my body, to take me where I wanted to go. That's what I needed to feel happy and authentic, not a handful of crumpled fives in my bra.

Maybe, right now, you don't know what your truth is either. That's OK, because I promise you that one day it will become apparent to you, and when it does, you have a responsibility to yourself to listen to it. So many of us swallow our truths to make someone else happy. We do things to please other people, rather than ourselves, and that's dangerous for a diva. Do that, and you'll become part of someone else's chorus, rather than the lead in your own musical. In drag and in life, you must first know who you are in order to know where you need to go.

By the way, I had my tits done for a third time in 2002. I'd just finished breastfeeding my youngest daughter when I noticed one was looking a little floppy. So after extensive research, I went to a new doctor in LA, Dr. Robert Rey, aka *Dr. 90210*, and sure enough, I had a slow leak in one of my implants. I had to have surgery to fix them anyway, so before I went under, I asked the doctor to right the wrong from so many years before, and he finally did. Now, I have 550cc implants, which make me a respectable 36D. I love them. They're fun. But, you know what? If I could go back and give my nineteen-year-old self some advice, I'd tell her boobs do not make a woman. But they do make a great fashion accessory (especially when you pad them with cutlets, and point those babies so far north they'll guide Mary and Joseph to the manger).

RULE _no._ 15:

IF THERE'S A CROWD, WORK IT.

Whether you're in a cubicle or in a club, onstage or on television, every diva has to know how to work a crowd. Any crowd. No matter how big or small, drunk or sober, straight or gay, flat or fluffy. Why? Well, it's sure as hell not to massage your own ego. It's because you never know who is in that crowd or what they will one day mean to you. Your job is to command everyone's attention the moment you walk into a room and make every one of them feel special. If you can do that, you'll be able to accomplish anything you set your mind to.

I've worked all kinds of rooms in my life: teen clubs, dance clubs, arenas, even dank, basement-level, hot-oil wrestling rings. In each of those places I learned how to connect with my audience, and that skill has always served me well. In fact, it's what's led me to and through my illustrious seventeen-year career in radio—and even more important, it's what led me to my best friend, RuPaul. This is the story of how we came together. (*Professionally* speaking, you perv.)

It was February 1996. Seduction was over. S.O.U.L. S.Y.S.T.E.M. was over. My engagement to my roller-skating fiancé, Michael, was over. I felt like I was in danger of being over, but you know I wasn't about to go down without a fight. I'd moved back to the Upper West Side—Seventieth and Broadway—and I was living with my gorgeous stripper friend Debbie, who'd recently left Goldfingers to go work at this "classy" new strip club called Scores. Howard Stern never raved about Goldfingers on the radio, but every day he talked about Scores. As a result, Debbie was making five grand a *night*, and even though I couldn't will myself to take my clothes off at that club in Queens, stripping was once again looking like a promising career choice for me.

Just as I was about to swing my titties around the stripper pole of life, Laura, my best friend from high school (who, incidentally, is still my best friend today), called me up. "Have you heard this new radio station WKTU?" she said. "They're playing *all* of our songs. ALL OF THEM!" Now, I've been obsessed with listening to the radio since I was a kid. Every Saturday, I'd tune into Casey Kasem's American Top 40 Countdown and write down every single song on the list in order in my notebook as they played on the air. If I missed one, I'd listen to the entire show again when it was rebroadcast later that night. So, when I hung up the phone with Laura, I tuned my radio to 103.5-WKTU, and started listening—and then I kept listening for hours. It was like I'd fallen in love all over again, and though I'd never been a DJ, all I could think about was how I could get on that station and finally make my childhood obsession with radio turn into a career.

After twenty-four straight hours of listening to Exposé, Lil' Suzy, and George Lamond, I had a revelation. Working at WKTU was my destiny. Of course, the station owners didn't know that yet, but I did. So, I worked every connection I could think of from my Seduction days, just to get a shot at an audition. I spent the next week, first looking up and then calling every DJ who'd ever interviewed me just to ask if they happened to have any contacts at this new station. No one did. I dialed dead end after dead end after dead end. Shit.

Then one morning, my roommate, Debbie came home from her shift at the club. It was ten a.m., and I was sulking on the couch. "Hey, so you know that radio station you want to be on?" she said, like it was no big deal. "I think my manager at Scores is going to work there. I'll check for you tonight." Her boss, it turns out, was "Goumba Johnny" Sialiano, who had just gotten himself hired to write for DJ Sean "Hollywood" Hamilton. I basically freaked when she told me that, and when she saw how excited I was, she went to work that night and scored me a meeting with Hollywood and Goumba at the club the next night.

If you don't already know this about me, then you should know this now: I'm a closer. I'm the f*cking Mariano Rivera of interviews. (He's a Yankee pitcher, nay, THE Yankee pitcher, if you don't know him. That's a *baseball* team, not a candle, queen.) If I can just get the chance to get in the game, I will always bring home a win. And Debbie is the one who got me in the radio game. Who would've ever thought I would've gotten my big break in radio from a stripper? Fine, maybe you would've, but I didn't. And

Ru and I on the set of the VH1 hit show *The RuPaul Show*.

At my wedding weekend with my biological mother, Joanne. We got married on a cruise ship.

Doing one of our infamous sketches on *The RuPaul Show*. I was playing a stripper.

I loved our min pin, Foxy.

On the set of *The RuPaul Show*.

Hosting our yearly sold out event for radio
station WKTU at Madison Square Garden
called *Miracle on 34th St*. This year featured
Cher and J Lo as headliners.

With my husband David on location in LA shooting *The RuPaul Show.*

Honeymooning in St. Lucia.

After our first dance as husband and wife, hubby went to eat and Ru and I danced all night!

Our cruise ship wedding.

The best daddy ever.
I couldn't imagine what my
girls would be like without him.
Look at the love and trust.

True love . . . me with Ru and Georges in 1997.

Ru, me, and Jody Watley at WKTU.

Ru and I broadcasting together for our
first week ever. The rest is herstory.

The best directors money could buy. Ru and
I directing the "Shakesqueer" challenge.

Delivering the final challenge in the Werkroom.

The final episode of *RuPaul's Drag Race* Season 7. The lady shines in red.

that's, by the way, why you work every crowd and never look down your overcontoured Magnolia Crawford nose at anyone. *Everyone* can help you. Every day, I thank my lucky stars for Debbie, her giant knockers, and her generosity.

As you may have guessed, after a night of gabbing with Goumba and Hollywood at Scores, they hired me in my first-ever paid radio gig: their Girl on the Street. I spent the next week in the most random places, including the Tick Tock Diner on Route 3 in Clifton, New Jersey, and the parking lot of a bar on Eighty-sixth Street in Bensonhurst, Brooklyn, handing out WKTU T-shirts and feeling amazing because: a) I was paying my radio dues, and b) even though I already knew I was, they thought I was good enough to be on the air with them! Talking to strangers with a microphone in my hand and getting them excited felt so natural to me, because it's what I'd done at Goldfingers for so long. I was so good at it that the following week, the station asked me to come into the studio and do the traffic reports. I had no idea what I was doing with that, but somehow I managed to deliver the copy but also insert jokes ("car-be-que" instead of a car fire, and other winners like that) and I stayed in that sweet spot, until they shifted me yet again. This time, they paired me with this crazy egomaniac named "Magic" Matt Alan. I am pretty sure he did not want me as his sidekick, but the station managers did, so he was forced to tolerate me. Tolerate me he did: We ended up getting along quite well, and he told me he thought I had talent. He also did a show about cigars on AM radio and brought me on to cohost a day with him on there too.

See? I told you I can work any room. I mean, WTF do I know about friggin' *cigars*?!

When I say you've got to know how to work any crowd to be successful, that also includes a crowd of one. Sometimes, if you pretend to like someone long enough, you find that you start to find things to really like about them, even if they're an egomaniac like Magic Matt. But here's the real T on working an egomaniac: Stoop down. Pretend you think you're way beneath them. Act incredibly interested in every word that passes their lips, even if you don't give a f*ck what they're saying. Eventually they'll rely on you to feed their ego. They'll find themself needing your praise, and when you reach that point—boom!—you'll be the one with all the power. (That's called "topping from below." And that's not about baseball. But you already know that, queen.)

By the end of that week. Magic and I were LIKE BUTTAH. But the auditions weren't over. The next week they were bringing in a NYC radio heavy hitter named "Broadway" Bill Lee. Now, Bill was a one-man show. He was known for rhyming while deejaying, and he was a ball of energy. He wasn't interested in having me as his sidekick. He wanted another girl, Lisa Taylor, an experienced radio girl who was on the station when it played country music. I was gutted. I was doing so well that I didn't want to lose momentum, but I had no choice but to sit back and let her audition for my role for the next week. I sat back and listened with a discriminatory ear, critiquing every word that came out of her mouth and interjecting my own punch lines from my apartment. Guess what? The bosses called

THE DIVA RULES

me up again once his audition week was up. Fashion Week was coming, and they wanted to try me with yet a different partner, one who already had a show on VH1. His name was—you guessed it—RuPaul.

I hadn't seen Ru at all since 1992, when we were both performing at a radio expo in New York. I was there to sing "It's Gonna Be a Lovely Day," and he'd just blown the eff up with "Supermodel." I remember the moment distinctly. I'd just walked into the green room in my full-lace bodysuit with nothing but a bra and G-string on underneath when I spotted him across the way. I'd watched Ru in the clubs for years, but I'd always admired him from afar. We were acquaintances, not friends, so I felt a little shy. Still, I steeled my nerves and approached him: "Hey, I don't know if you remember me or not," and he takes one look at me and goes, "Bitch, stop right there. I used to watch your little blond ass bop all around at the Red Zone. I kept my eye on you for years! You're a f*cking superstar!" He actually said that shit to me. I was like, "Oh my God! Really? Go on!"

When they put us together for Fashion Week in 1996, I was the first to arrive at WKTU's studios in Jersey City. I had no idea what he thought of being—surprise!—paired with yours truly, and I remember just sitting there, waiting for Ru to show up. When he walked in and saw my familiar visage, a big grin spread across his face. He threw open his arms for a hug, and as he squeezed me hello, he said, "*Of course*, it's you. Of course, you're the one sitting right here. You have more f*cking lives in you than anyone I know."

That week on the radio, we had more fun together than any two humans should ever be allowed. They'd paired us with a New York radio legend, "Fast Freddie" Colon, whom I used to listen to when I was a kid. He was our straight man, and they let us be complete animals. To this day, when I look back on that first week together, I think (and I know Ru would agree) that it was the best time of our lives. We were so damn good together. In fact, we did so well together that we beat Howard Stern for the top ratings spot that month, and that, my friends, is HUGE.

And that was it. WKTU made us the permanent cohosts of the coveted morning-drive slot. And after that, Ru brought me in as his sidekick on his VH1 show, *The RuPaul Show*, where I played Ed McMahon to his Johnny Carson, only he let me shine way more than Johnny ever let Ed. My favorite part of the show was when he let me open with a segment we called "Mission Visage," which was a *Candid Camera*–style hidden-camera prank, where I'd get to punk an unsuspecting person. To this day, Ru and I still talk about that show. That conversation usually ends with him saying, "Bitch, we are not done with that." Consider yourself warned.

I felt like I had found my true home behind the microphone. So, even after Ru left radio to move to LA and focus on acting and other ventures, I stayed on the air in New York, then Los Angeles, then New York again, then West Palm Beach, and finally Miami— for a total of seventeen straight years. I've lived my whole life on the radio. I got married on the radio. I gave birth to my first daughter on the air. Literally. I had a C-section, and I was hold-ing a microphone before and immediately after my sweet baby girl arrived. There's a scene in Madonna's *Truth or Dare* in which Warren Beatty grumbles, "She doesn't want to live off camera, much less talk. There's nothing to say off camera. Why would you say something if it's off camera? What point is there existing?" I live my life, out loud, with a microphone in my hand, and I've always shared everything with my listeners. Why? Because I respect them too much not to. That, and I'm an idiot. But, I feel like if they're getting up every day, tuning in, and making me a part of their lives, I want them to be a part of my life too.

Which all goes back to working the crowd and connecting with people. It's what I do best, and it's been one of the cornerstones of my success. So, how do you do it—and do it well?

Here's the T:

THE

T

THE DOS AND OH-NO-SHE-BETTER-DON'TS OF WORKING A CROWD:

DON'T ACT DESPERATE: That's a big no-no. If you're trying too hard, you come across as needy, and nobody is endeared to desperation. Instead, pull attention to yourself without crossing the line into obnoxious territory. Where's that line? You'll know it if you cross it. Be charming. Be charismatic. Be grand. And laugh at other people's jokes; it'll help you come across as confident.

DON'T GO IT ALONE: The moment you walk into a room, try to find a person you know so you're at least not standing alone. It's just harder to work a room by your-self. Having someone by your side, even if you don't really want to hang out together, can give you both a little sense of much-needed security.

DON'T TALK POLITICS OR RELIGION: It has no place at a party or at work or, take it from me, in discussions with your mother-in-law. It just never ends well, so don't even start.

DON'T LINGER TOO LONG: Leave everybody wanting more of you. If you finally get into a conversation with the person you've been most eager to talk to—a potential boss, a cast-ing director, a crush—politely excuse yourself while your banter is still going strong. You want them to feel disap-pointed that you left them, not happy that you're gone. And if you ever get cornered in a boring conversation, do not stay in it, because you could be missing something better. My exit strategy is always, "Excuse me, I have to use the bathroom." Never say you're getting a drink, because they'll probably follow you to the bar.

DON'T ACT SUPERIOR, MAMA: You're really not. Divas know there's always somebody else to impress. And if you can connect with anyone, you can belong anywhere.

DO VISUALIZE SUCCESS: Before you head out to a party, job interview, audition, or performance, spend five to ten minutes alone picturing what it'll look like when you pull it off flawlessly. When you can see yourself succeeding, it only becomes that much easier to actually do it. All of my friends know that I need to be alone in my dressing room before any performance. I spend that time running my lines. It just helps get me in a positive mind-set and makes me feel like I've got a handle on what I need to do.

DO MAKE AN ENTRANCE: I'm a Virgo, which means I'm always early or on time, but when I want to work a crowd, I show up a little late. I'm not talking an hour late, because I'm not an asshole. I'm talking five to ten minutes late. That way, everybody is waiting for me to arrive. Or, at least in my head they are, and that helps inflate my feelings of self-importance. Try it. It works.

DO READ THE ROOM: You've got to be acutely aware of what's going on around you so you can match the energy of the room. Are people eating hors d'oeurves? Are they kiki'ing? What's the talk of the night? You've got to feel it out, so you can calibrate yourself.

DO MAKE EVERYONE FEEL SPECIAL: There's just no good reason to make anyone else feel bad, so do what you can to try to make everyone around you feel good. They may not remember what you say to them, but they will remember how you made them feel. (This holds true for social media too. My own personal rule: I try to respond to everyone, because I get it. I'm a fan too. What I don't get is why the f*ck people like Zac Efron have a Twitter, when they so obviously don't do the upkeep themselves? For better or worse, people are talking to me, and I want them to know I'm listening and I'm human.)

DO KNOW THAT NO ONE IS BETTER THAN YOU: The only difference between me and you is that most likely, I have bigger tits (that goes for most of the men reading this as well). But, those superficial things aside, we are all the same. Everybody is important. Some people just project that more. Be one of those people.

RULE _no._ 16:

FRIEND UP.

I've just recently celebrated the seventeenth anniversary of my twenty-ninth birthday, which means, children, I've picked up a little bit of wisdom over the years. And what I've learned is that people tend to choose their friends for one of two reasons: 1) They make you feel better because you're you or 2) they make you feel better because you're not them. And let me tell you right now, the latter is shit. While it's admittedly sometimes appealing, especially in moments of insecurity, to surround yourself with the most nonthreatening people you can imagine, it is not what real divas do. You can't become a diva by default, just because you're the sparkliest one of a dull bunch, the only diamond among cubic zirconia, the only Louboutin among Payless. Everyone will see through that and, more important, so will you. No, instead, divas seek out fabulousness. We are on it like it's the warehouse sale at Barney's. If it exists within a 120-mile radius of us, we _will_ find it. Why? Because to be as grand as we are, we're in constant need of inspiration. We need to lift each other up. Alone, we are fierce. Together, we're on fi-yah.

That is certainly true of Ru and me. When I first saw him back in the clubs, I was completely drawn to him, but honestly, just a bit too intimidated to approach him. I don't know why. It could've been that I was only a kid, barely eighteen, and he had a little more life experience under his wig, or it could've been his microscopic miniskirt, his big afro, his even bigger personality, or the fact that he was an intimidating seven feet tall in drag. Of course, I had a *load* of queens in my life at the time—after all, I was hanging out with the best of the lot in the ballrooms—but I also sensed instantly that there was just something special about Ru. He rules every room he enters, the millisecond he enters it. He just effortlessly owns everyone's attention, and once he gets it, he doesn't just suck it up. Instead, he's like this spectacular prism, reflecting and refracting all that light and love right back at everyone around him. His gift is hard to explain, other than saying this: As fabulous and as beautiful as he is, when you're in his presence, *you* suddenly feel more beautiful too.

I *had* to know him. I didn't know how we'd become friends, especially given that I could only muster a "hey, girl" in passing in the clubs, but call it intuition, I just knew instinctively that one day, when the time was right, we somehow would get to know each other.

So it was kismet when, in 1996, we were serendipitously paired up professionally for the first time on New York City's brand-new powerhouse radio station, WKTU. That on-air coupling was the start of our lifelong relationship. We became not only instant coworkers, but also instant friends. Our show was broadcast out of a little studio in Jersey City, and since we hosted the morning drive, we had to be there at the ungodly hour of four a.m. every Monday through Friday. Since I was living on Manhattan's Upper West Side, that meant I had to wake up at two a.m. and leave my little apartment by three a.m. to brave the empty-except-for-rapists subway, and then the PATH train, to Jersey. Ru, however, did not. He was the star of the show, so the station sent a town car for him everyday. It'd wait at his front door in the Village to pick him up and after we'd finished, his driver would drop him back home. Nobody at the station gave a shit if I was riding public transit alone in the middle of the night, but the moment Ru found out, he put an end to it immediately. "Oh no, girl," he said. "You're going to take my car." And that was it. From day two onward, Ru sent his fancy black car and driver to pick me up on our way to work every single day: me first, him second (ahem, like a true gentleman). And in the wee hours of all those mornings, and later in the girls' room at the station, and even later after the radio show ended when we'd both go to VH1 to tape *The RuPaul Show*, we'd gossip and kiki, just as we did on the radio and television, and like we still do today. Literally for two years straight, when we weren't sleeping, Ru and I were together. Our bond was forged then, and to this day, it's unbreakable.

We have a strict no-bullshit policy in our friendship. We know each other better than anyone else, and we never pretend to be—or feel like we have to even pretend to be—people we're not. And he's seen me through some bad shit too. When we started our radio show together, I'd been dating this guy, a stripper by night, psychology PhD student by day named Michael (not to be confused with my ex-fiancé, Michael). We'd been together for four years, and I thought I was going to spend the rest of my life with him. He was one of my great loves. And then, one day in May 1996, out of the blue, he called up and broke up with me over the phone. Just like that. Never saw him again. It was torture for me as my heart was shattered beyond recognition.

That summer, fueled by my devastating heartbreak, I went on a rampage of pure debauchery. I was doing weekend radio gigs at the Jersey shore, and when I was there, I'd basically pick up the hottest flavor-of-the-moment and have my way with anybody who was DTF. My heart was so destroyed that I was just trying to forget everything. Or at least, just Michael. After each of my Saturday night conquests, I'd coldly kick the guy—or girl—or both—out of bed and never talk to them again. I was treating them like I'd seen so many guys treat my girlfriends, and trust me, it didn't make me proud. I was being a heartless, selfish dude. And come Monday, when Ru and I were driving in his town car to work, I'd tell him all about what I'd done. He was in a different place from me. When he started getting clean, he evolved spiritually, and after hearing too many of my stories, he eventually gave me a copy of *A Return to Love* by Marianne Williamson. I'm not into self-help books, but when The World's Most Famous Drag Queen gives you one, you read it. I devoured that one and I'd call him the moment I finished every chapter. I remember one day standing on Sixty-eighth Street, dialing his number and just unleashing this torrent of emotion the moment he answered: "Oh my god! This chapter where she talks about how people come into your life for different amount of times for different purposes?" And he'd just say, "I told you, girl. I know."

Whenever I fell, Ru was always there to pick me up. When I moved to Los Angeles in 2011, after getting fired from my six-figure radio gig in West Palm Beach (more on that later), the only thing I had going for me was *Drag Race*. Sure, it was something, but the show was still fairly new, and the money I was making from it was not enough to support my family of four. (After all, we only taped for four weeks out of the year.) My husband was home, raising our kids, so it was up to me to put food on the table, clothes on our backs, gas in the car, and at this point in my life the pressure

THE

IF I HAD ONE WISH FOR YOU, it would be that you're blessed with a solid-gold friend as wonderful, loyal, supportive, and fabulous as Ru. Remember, it's quality, not quantity, and soul mates aren't only lovers. Now, I hear you asking me, "Michelle, how do you meet him or her?" Here's my advice: Find the most fabulous person in the room and have the guts to get to know him. The person you're drawn to and don't know why. Even if you never sleep with him or her, you'll learn something, and so will they. And, who knows, if you're ridiculously lucky, some twenty-five years later, you two could even be starring on a TV show together. #Blessed nearly broke me. I felt lost. I was trying my hardest to make shit happen, but it just wasn't and I didn't know how to change that fact. I remember meeting Ru one day for lunch, and I just broke down in his arms. I'm not usually a crier, but with tears streaming down my face, I told him, "I just don't know what to do." He put his hands on my shoulders, looked me in the eyes, and said, "Michelle, you are the most resilient person I know. You have never been let down by this universe. You will never fail. It's not in your cards. You just have to know what you want to do, and then you have to do it. You, my friend, are a f*cking star, and we both know you've got what it takes." By the end of the conversation, we were both crying, but he'd said exactly what I needed to hear, and knowing he believed in me in my weakest moment helped me believe in myself. I always walk away from him feeling more confident.

And he, too, knows that I will never let him down. I know some people say I ride his coattails, but the truth is, we are better together than we are alone, at least from where I'm sitting. I'm the Ethel to his Lucy, the Flo to his Alice, the Rhoda to his Mary. Nobody can deliver him quite like I can, and I will always be there to do it—on air, off air, under water, in space, wherever he needs me.

Ru and I have grown up together. We've watched each other fall in love. We've watched each other become mothers—me to my two daughters and him to an entire community of young drag queens. We've helped each other through the darkest times and happiest times, and we've become each other's partners in both work and in life. I love him more deeply than I knew possible, and I know he loves me too.

RULE *no.* 17:

SCREW THE PENIS CLUB.
(Figuratively speaking, darling.)

File under maddening but true: Our world is ruled by a not-so-secret, informal organization that has no official name but which I like to call The Penis Club. The only membership requirement: a dick. (To be clear, you just have to have one, you don't have to *be* one. Although it's amazing how often these two things coincide.) And boys, listen up, because for some reason, if you *do* have a penis but are not regularly sticking it into a biological female, your Penis Club membership is only second-tier, so much of this applies to you too. Anyway, anyone who does not fulfill the aforementioned membership requirement is automatically punished accordingly, mostly through exclusion from opportunity, economic penalties, harassment, condescension, and other totally f*cked-up, annoying, and often arbitrary means. There's one more catch: If you dare mention the existence of this club or challenge its rules, you will automatically be branded a raving bitch.

I'm not being dramatic. I mean, I WOULD NEVER. I'm just speaking the cold, hard truth. Sexism is alive and well. It doesn't matter which field you're in—finance, law, medicine, marketing, media, whatever—you, as a woman, will make less money than your male coworkers, especially the straight white ones. And to earn the paycheck you do bring home, you'll have to work, if not longer and harder, then smarter for it. Don't get me wrong here: I love me some good male domination. I just prefer it in my bedroom, not my workplace.

I spent nearly two decades working in radio, one of the most male-dominated industries in America. It's been dude domain forever, even long before *WKRP in Cincinnati* cemented the idea in our heads that men are made to be DJs while women are more suited to looking like Loni Anderson, working behind a desk, and pushing papers. (Her hair, though! I would've killed to have had it!) In my own seventeen years on air, the only other women out there who found success doing what I was doing were Angie Martinez, Miss Jones, and my mentor-in-my-head, Wendy Williams, whom I used to listen to growing up. Soon after I got on the air, people even started calling me The White Wendy Williams. The four of us? We were *it*, the only busty broads holding our own among all-male station owners, program directors, and DJs.

People thought I'd fail. No one thought a female DJ could win as many hearts (or ears) as a male one. So, as you might imagine, it quickly became my mission to prove everyone around me wrong. I could do everything the men could do, and not only could I do it, but I could do it better. Look, you're not going to topple the patriarchy, but you can learn how to work within it until things do change, or you make them change. Here's the T on how to use your diva strengths to gain power and kick ass in a male-dominated field:

Accept every challenge

When I started on the radio, I started at the bottom, but I vowed to do whatever it took to work my way to the top. For my first job at WKTU in 1996, I was getting paid $55,000 a year, the union mandated dirt minimum, even though Ru and I were the top-rated, most-listened-to radio team in NYC. We were literally the number one show in the number one market, and we successfully dethroned the king of all media and my favorite radio personality in the history of ever, Howard Stern, in our first ratings book. Even so, at the time, Howard was probably making upward of two million bucks a year, and I was earning pocket change. Did I get a raise? Nope. Did I ask for one? I didn't dare. At the time, I wasn't exactly panicked, but I was incredibly driven to make this radio thing work. My money from *The Bodyguard* (Track 9, baby!) had run dry, after I bought my parents a house and car, and my brother a car, and, it probably needs to be said, myself about a million pieces of Diamonique from QVC. And I was so much happier sitting behind a microphone with Ru than I knew I would've been had I been twirling my titties at Scores. I wasn't being paid what the ratings showed I was worth, but I took it as a challenge to prove myself until they either ponied up or someone else poached me.

By the way, that pay inequity has persisted throughout my career. I always try not to talk about money with my colleagues, but it would come up every now and again, and whenever it did, I always discovered I was always doing more work for less money. Sometimes I made a stink about it. Sometimes I didn't. I'll only take on challenges I know I can win. You'll never see me competing with anyone in a chin-up contest or a turtleneck fashion show, but if you want to try to outtalk me, I know for a fact that you will lose. I've been given the gift of gab. I can entertain *anyone* with my mouth. (Get your mind out of the gutter, girl. You know what I mean.) And once I got on the air, there was just no stopping me.

Be the first one in the office every day

In every major market I worked—New York, LA, Miami—I always anchored the coveted morning-drive slot. And I'm proud to say that every single day of my career, I was always the first one in the office. If we went on air at six a.m., I was there at four a.m. If we went on at five a.m., I'd arrive at the studio by three-thirty a.m., even if that meant I had to set my alarm for two a.m. I wasn't there to put in face time. After all, all of my coworkers and bosses were home in bed, so no one else was even there to appreciate my presence. I used all those extra hours to prep. I did a segment called "The Scoop," which was a celebrity gossip bit. When I started radio, that segment was seven minutes long with lots of interactive banter, which is an eternity on the radio. I started radio before the Internet was used for resources other than checking your AOL, so every Thursday, I'd go to the newsstands to pick up the *Enquirer*, the *Sun*, and *Star* magazine, and I'd try to plot how I could make the gossip in them last a week. By day five, I'd inevitably be talking about somebody's dog, but it didn't matter. The segment was a hit. I was good at it, because I put the extra work in to be good at it. And because I worked just as hard if not harder and longer than my male cohosts, every single time that on-air sign lit up, I knew I was more prepared than anyone else in the room. That made me better at my job than everyone else in the room too. Plus, it gave me the confidence to keep reaching higher.

Find the good guys

Just because it's a big boys' club out there, that doesn't mean there aren't some truly fantastically amazing members of it. Goumba Johnny and Hollywood Hamilton, the first guys I worked with at WKTU as their "girl on the street," taught me tons about radio. I came in knowing nothing. That egomaniacal crazy dude, Magic Matt, whom I hated at first but grew to love, helped me get a radio agent so I could renegotiate my contracts. And when, after six years on the air, WKTU declined to renew my contract ("flat ratings," they said) four days before Christmas and when I was seven months pregnant, Goumba immediately picked up the phone and helped me get an audition for a gig in LA. I landed it on the spot, and two months later, when my second daughter, Lola, was only nine days old, I moved my family to sunny California, where I cohosted the morning drive with Sinbad for six months. When he decided that morning radio was not the right fit for a comic who does shows at night, he quit and I carried the show on my own for another six months, and then my radio dream came true: They let me have a female cohost. Any man in radio will try to tell you why the female/female morning shows never work, but luckily my talented cohost Diana Steele and I got to prove all the big boys wrong. We kicked butt on the morning drive in Los Angeles together for two and a half years before said big boys fired our amazing female program director to bring in a male one. His first priority? Split up our all-female morning show by adding a male. That male was Mario Lopez, the cutest guy ever, but almost too sweet to be my dream cohost. I am way more of a Howard Stern type of chick, so, later, in 2005, when Mix 102.7 came calling with radio legend and my real radio mentor, Frankie Blue, at the helm, you better believe they were able to lure me home. They also lured me with a repairing of RuPaul and myself in AM drive again, just as in the old WKTU days. Tripling my salary helped too. Which is all to say, there are good guys out there who will recognize you for your talent, not your tits. They'll want to help you because it's the right thing to do, and when they offer, the smartest thing you can do is accept.

Do what it takes to get shit done

First of all, when I say screw The Penis Club, I want to reiterate that I do *not* mean literally having sex with them. Screwing your boss (or all the men in your office) is sure as hell not the way to earn respect. Instead, you've got to be smarter about it. Read the room. Figure out what, or whom, you're up against. Then plan your fight strategy. As you watch far less talented men repeatedly get promoted faster than you, and you learn that those below you are earning more than you, you may feel the overwhelming desire to become a raging bitch. I get that. And you know what? That works for some women. Wendy Williams has a famously low tolerance for sexist bullshit and a famously hot temper when she calls someone on it. This has undoubtedly helped her in her career. I tend to take a different tack. I schmooze, using my feminine wiles. Is it manipulative? Hell to the yeah! What's wrong with that? I see nothing wrong with it. It's one tool I have in my arsenal that no guy can either withstand or compete with. So, when a program director tells me I have to play twelve songs in an hour, leaving me zero time to do my thing on air, I will not hesitate to put on a low-cut shirt, walk into his office, and ask in my sweetest voice, "Please let me show you what I can do with eight songs. Won't you just let me try it?" A diva does what she needs to do get the shit done. You don't have to be a bitch, though I fully support you if you want to go that route. You just cannot be passive.

Stay true to yourself

I've watched some women actually try to join The Penis Club. They just start pretending they're one of the guys, as if taking up golf and dressing in a suit will magically make their pay gap disappear. It's a mistake. Not only will it not help you, but you may lose yourself in the process. Had I done that, I could've been some sort of asshole shock jock, but it's not me. Instead, I stayed true to who I was. For example, I covered my headphones with pink fur and crystals, so if anyone walked into my studio, they knew who they were getting right away. I hung a sign on my office wall

THE

TOPPLING THE PENIS CLUB is all about perseverance, sticking it out. When you're faced with year after year of sexist bullshit, it's easy to get discouraged. In fact, a lot of women will get so worn down that they quit. They walk away from their dreams, disillusioned, saying they can't take it anymore. They're just not cut out for it. But let me ask you this: How the hell are you going to prove yourself if you just give up like that? I know it sucks that you have to prove yourself all the time, but you do. And you can. You've got what it takes to succeed, and once you get that through your gorgeous head, no one can take that away from you. Now, diva, get out there and show me your stuff.

that said, "What would Madonna do?" I wore my leopard prints to work every day. Every boss I've ever had has seen my headphones and has said, "*Of course* you have pink fuzzy headphones," and that was it. I love that I am who I am, and everyone else should too.

Help a sister out

Oddly, the first radio relationship I ever forged was with a radio chick who tragically went by the name of Powermouth Patty. She auditioned for the gig with WKTU, and I beat her out for it. When I landed the gig, she called me up and said, "You are so good. I just wanted you to know that." She didn't have to do that. Most people never would, and yet I'll never forget her for it. She even went on to give me some great advice in general about the radio biz. Women generally don't help other women in business out, and I think it's a travesty. And I understand why it happens. We're all constantly being pushed to the bottom, and we're worried that if we use our one magic bullet to help a friend, we won't have that favor to call in when we need it for ourselves. But by not helping one another, we're actually hurting one another, and ultimately ourselves. There is room for more than one woman to be successful. There is room for all of us at the top. We just need to stick together. We need to be one another's allies. We need to lift one another up.

RULE _no._ 18:

NEVER TRUST A MAN IN DOCKERS.

You certainly can't tell everything about a man by the way he dresses, but you can tell some things. For example, if he's wearing pleated, wrinkle-free khakis, belted so high above his belly button that you can see his moose knuckle, you can be almost certain that he's kinky as hell (which normally I'd say is a good thing, but not necessarily here) and his mind is utterly void of creativity. After all, there are a lot of different ways to look professional in an office, and Dockers are the most disconcertingly nondescript option. I guarantee you, the guys who wear these pants are the same ones who call _Two and a Half Men_ their favorite TV show of all time. Real-life translation: They basically worship maleness above all else, even when it's grotesquely mediocre. Therefore, what I'm telling you, divas, is that when you see a man wearing these hiked-up pants, just proceed with caution. That's all.

And to be clear, this is not about me being a fashion snob, because I'm not one at all. (Hello, I get half my wardrobe at Hot Topic and Forever 21 wedged right between the Orange Julius and Auntie Anne's Pretzels in the mall!) It's about reading the signs people are giving you and using them to inform the way you move forward. I certainly don't expect every man to look as sharp as Ru does, when he dresses in a suit and visits the *Drag Race* workroom. (By the way, he looks that good *all* the time, even when he's in his trackies.) I just appreciate a man who chooses an actual style and owns it. If he's a dandy, fab. If he's a slob, also fab. At least it's a choice. One of my favorite radio bosses of all time was a gay man with a nose job (love), a porn mustache (love), bonded teeth (love), and a toupee (OMG yes), and he wore a flannel shirt to work every single day. I loved everything about his look, even the flannel, because at least it was interesting. A gay in a flannel is always an enigma, and I love a good puzzle. A straightie in wrinkle-free khakis never is. You pretty much know whom you're getting, and it's rarely someone as sparkly or rule-breaking as you may prefer.

I learned this from my time at SUNNY 104.3 in West Palm Beach. Working in radio is a little like working for the military in that you're constantly picking up your entire family and moving to where you're needed. Or just, you know, wanted. In radio, every December, all the DJs anxiously wait to see if their contracts will be renewed. And if they are, hooray, you stay put another year. If they're not, then it's "Honey, list the house and pack up the kids. We're heading west. Or north. Or south. Or somewhere else that's not here." In 2007, a year after my short stint at the identity-crisis-plagued Mix 102.7 in New York City, I was offered something I'd never had before: a *five*-year radio contract in West Palm Beach. I had one daughter in second grade and another in preschool, and a five-year gig meant that for once my kids could make—and *keep*—some friends for a little while, so I jumped on it. At last, I could give my family some sweet, sweet stability.

West Palm Beach had fewer listeners than I had in New York or LA, but I loved it there, and I was still pulling in a solid six figures. And I knew so many New Yorkers who'd moved down there that I felt like it was the sixth borough of NYC, only with palm trees and without MetroCards, two major plusses in my book. The station's general manager was a guy named Lee Strasser, a real old-fashioned radio guy who believed in talent. He loved everything about the format, and I loved everything about him. To make our bond even stronger? He was a Jersey boy. After I finished doing the morning drive every weekday, I'd go sit in his office and we'd just shoot the shit and laugh and laugh together.

By 2008, to everyone's shock and dismay, Lee was let go after twenty-two freakin' years of hard work and devotion, and they brought in a heartless numbers guy from Minnesota. He looked like an overweight Bill Murray with a thinning flattop, and liter-ally *every* single day he wore tan Dockers to the office. I swear the guy must've had forty pairs of the same exact boring pants, which, at the time, I noticed enough to clock, but that's about all. Anyway, despite his uninspired fashion, he wrote inspiring mass emails. (Yes, emails, which, in retrospect, now seems so shockingly impersonal.) He somehow convinced us all that there was more money to be had in sunny Florida, and if we just followed him, we'd all find it together. Dockers wanted us to believe that he was our messiah, and for a very short while, we all became his hopeful disciples.

In retrospect, I wish I'd paid closer attention to the clues he was sending that something was just not right about him. There were other warning signs. Like, I was one of his biggest talents, and he never once met with me in person, or as far as I know, with any of the other on-air personalities. I worked with him for months, and I'd never once been in his office. And soon enough, the promises he'd made to us about gaining bigger numbers started to crumble. "Stay positive," he'd tell us. "It's just going to get better." And then one day in passing, my extremely talented, wonderful (and so wonderfully wholesome that I used to call him "Beav" as in *Leave it to Beaver*) morning-drive cohost, Rick Shockley, mentioned that he saw Dockers at his church, and I was actually relieved by this news. I thought, *OK, he may not be in touch with his fashion sense or maybe even with the realities of running a radio station, but he's in touch with his spirituality. That's good.* (Whether you worship Jesus, Allah, or a tree, it doesn't matter to me. It's just nice to be able to release your drama to someone or something.)

Then, one day out of the blue, I got a phone call that changed my life. Or, at least, should have. I was sitting in the driveway of a teacher's house, waiting for my daughter to finish her math-tutoring session inside, when I answered the call. It was Randy Barbato from World of Wonder on the other end. He was an old, dear friend. My former manager and he (and his company) produced *The RuPaul Show* on VH1, where I had *the* best time of my life. He said, "Look, Michelle. We're trying out this new show with Ru called *RuPaul's Drag Race*. It's not a lot of money, but it's got huge potential." He did not have to say another word to convince me to work with my best friend again. I was so in.

Now, as a rule, if you work in radio and your first name isn't Howard and your last name isn't Stern, then you get exactly two weeks off a year, and not in succession. To tape season one of *Drag Race*, I'd have needed three weeks. So I made a foolproof plan in my head, and then I made an appointment with Dockers to discuss the opportunity. It was my first time in his office, and when I walked in, my heart was suddenly beating out of my chest. Authority figures always make me a bit nervous. I'm a pleaser, so maybe "anxious" is a better word. Hello? I'm a Virgo, and we like everyone to be happy at all times. So, I just took a deep breath and said, "Listen, I have this opportunity that I'd really like to pursue. Do you know who RuPaul is?" He nodded, but I wasn't even sure if he heard me; still, I went on. "Well, Ru and I worked together for years on TV and radio, and he's got another TV show that he wants me to do with him. It'll only take three weeks to tape, but it's in LA. I'm not asking for any time off at all. I can wake up at three a.m. and do the morning-drive show live every day with Rick via ISDN line. No one would ever know I wasn't sitting right next to him in the studio." Dockers waited until I finished, and then said, "I'm going to have to say no." That's it. Just "no." I protested, "What? You didn't even think about it for a second." He said, "OK, I'll think about it more and let you know tomorrow morning."

WHEN I TELL YOU TO NEVER TRUST A MAN IN DOCKERS, it's just my way of saying that you should always try to get a read on people sooner, rather than later. Every man in nondescript khakis surely isn't an asshole, but if you find something about someone that unsettles you or makes you feel like something is just slightly off, even if you don't know what that something is yet and even if you otherwise like the guy, put a pin in it and stick it to the bulletin board in your mind. Listen to your gut, because your instincts are never wrong. In work and life, give everyone the benefit of the doubt, but keep your trust until you're sure it's been duly earned.

I didn't sleep at all that night, but I couldn't figure out a plausible reason why he would say no. If it was good for me, it'd also be good for the station, especially if the show took off the way everyone thought it would. So the next morning, after my show ended, Dockers called me down to his office. He said, "I still have to say no." And that was it. I was stunned. "Can you tell me why?" I said, to which he responded, "I just don't think it's the right image for our station." I just stood there, staring at him with my jaw on the floor. "You've got to be kidding me!" I snapped. And he just started pecking at his computer's keyboard, pretending that I wasn't still in the room. Eventually, I turned on my heels and stormed out of his office. I made it to my car before I burst into tears. Dockers single-handedly crushed my dreams and there was nothing I could do about it as I was in the beginning stages of a five-year contract, bound to this hateful asshat.

Because I'm the sole breadwinner in my family, there was no way I could risk getting fired, so I called Randy at World of Wonder and broke the terrible news to him: I was out. The show would have to go on without me. Even worse, I couldn't be there for my best friend, and that nearly killed me.

RULE _no._ 19:

PROJECT POSITIVITY, EVEN WHEN YOU FEEL LIKE SHIT.

There will be times in your life when nothing seems to go your way. You can do *everything* right—plan ahead, work hard, dream big, get straight, go forward, move ahead—and still get whipped. It's a lifelong struggle for most people, me included, to come to terms with the idea that, as much as we'd like to believe it, we are not really in control of everything in our lives. Some things, sure. But not *all* things. Like, for instance, other people.

When my boss at the West Palm Beach radio station told me that he would, under no circumstances, allow me to take my rightful seat next to Ru on season one of *Drag Race*, I was completely devastated. Ru did not take the news well either. He knew I was supposed to be a part of the show, he felt the blow of the reality that I wouldn't be able to join him every bit as much as I did. My absence caused the first (and only) real rift our relationship has ever seen. Ru is a Scorpio, which means when he's hurt, he just shuts down, so after I told Randy I couldn't do the show, I didn't hear from my best friend for a long, long time. It was the saddest, loneliest year of my life. I was gutted.

When season one of *Drag Race* finally aired, I forced myself to watch it in the same way you force yourself to get a dental cleaning. You know you need to and it will make you look and feel better, but you really don't want to because it makes you uncomfortable. I wanted to see Ru kick ass, and of course I was rooting for his success harder than anyone. And yet the show made me cringe, only because it was just so difficult to see another woman sitting in my seat. My seat! Now, at that point I didn't know Merle Ginsberg. Never even met her. But it was clear from Episode 1 that she wasn't me, and—no T, no shade—she could never be me. She was a sweet, pretty, straight fashionista, which is fine and lovely, but she lacked, in my opinion, the gay fabulosity that one needs sitting next to the Grand Dame on *RuPaul's Drag Race*. That and the fact she couldn't come close to delivering Ru like I could, but let's be honest, no one can, so it's not her fault. Meanwhile, I sat at home, sulking, feeling like a pathetic loser who apparently had so little power in the world that I just couldn't get off of work for three weeks. But that was the truth.

I strongly suspected that Ru was upset with me for turning the show, and therefore him, down. I'm talking upset at the depth of his soul, upset. After I broke the bad news, I'd tried to call him to talk it through. He never answered my calls. (*But* . . . to be fair, even if Dolly Parton herself called him, he probably still wouldn't answer his phone. He just never does. He absolutely hates cell phones and refuses to use one.) Still, hoping beyond hope, I left a message. And another. And another.

If I were a different person, this might be the point where I'd either blow up in anger or meltdown with grief, the latter being the road I usually travel down, but then I quickly reminded myself that this is not how divas do it. We keep it together. We stay positive, even when things get ugly, and we always try to act with grace and compassion. I knew Ru was being this way not because he was angry, but because he was hurt. I let him down. He needed to process that emotion, and everyone knows you don't kick a queen when she's down, especially the fiercest queen in the world. So, with that in mind, I took a breath and wrote a simple email saying, "I love you. I'm so happy for your success." And after what felt like an eternity, but in actuality was only a few days, my best friend forgave me, and Ru and I were able to repair our bruised hearts

THE

PEOPLE REMEMBER EVERYTHING. They always remember the bad more than the good, but when you're really good, they remember that too. So even in your darkest moments, live your life with love. You will be rewarded in more ways than you could ever count.

and our special relationship. There was no way anything was going to keep us apart.

When you're having a hard time yourself, or going through a hard time with someone else, always approach the situation with love and gratitude in your heart. That can be ridiculously difficult, especially when you feel rejected, lonely, wronged, or misunderstood, but trust me, girl, it's the only healthy way to move through this world. And by staying positive, you'll not only find more peace in your life, but good things will come to you: more friends, more success, more opportunities. Just look at some of these queens who are asked to sashay away on *Drag Race*. Kelly Mantle, Vivacious, Trinity K. Bonet and Joslyn Fox, all of season six, may not have won the crown, but they won our hearts because of the grace with which they carried themselves. Even when they were eliminated, which I'm sure cut them to the core, they stayed positive, thanked Ru, and walked away with their heads held high.

Now, compare them to Magnolia Crawford, who I do love and adore, but she projected the worst attitude from the start. Mark my words: If you are snarky, mean, and rude, and if you write nasty shit on the mirror of life or even just think it in your heart, you're never going to make it. You'll poison yourself with toxic emotion, and you'll poison every opportunity that may come your way. Blowing up. Melting down. Posting nasty things on Facebook or Twitter. Infighting. All those negative responses are the emotional equivalent of binging on junk food. It might feel good in the moment, but I guarantee you, it will make you feel like total shit later.

My idea of a headshot was very different from what the casting people were used to.

RULE *no.* 20:

ACT LIKE A STAR, EVEN IF NO ONE'S WATCHING.

When life takes a turn for the shitty and things stop going your way, it's really easy to just give up on yourself. One minute, you're all, "I'm the queeeeen of the world!" And then you get dumped, or fired, or rejected, or shut down, or whatever, and that shady little voice inside of your head, the one that stays silent in good times, starts telling you what's really what: You're nothing. No, you're less than nothing. You never deserved success or love anyway. Everything you've done so far? That was luck. Or better yet, a mistake. In fact, you should be embarrassed that you ever even thought for a second that you'd actually *earned* it. You're a failure. Worse, you're a fat failure with—gasp!—no fashion sense and bad hair.

Sound familiar? Yeah, we've all been there. Every single one of us engages in negative self-talk from time to time. And surrendering to this nasty chatter is harmful not only to a diva's career and relationships, but also to our hearts, both physically and emotionally. When you dwell on the negative, run your failures on an endless loop in your mind, it changes who you are. It can turn something only mildly rotten into something horrid, and it can rob you of everything from your confidence to your inner peace to your good health. Trust me, it's not worth it. You do not want to go there. I did, and it nearly killed me.

Drag Race went on for two grueling years without me, and the show was a raging success. Just to torture myself, I'd watch every single episode from my couch in Wellington, Florida, looking for solace in a bag of Flaming Hot Cheetos and feeling sorry for my total-loser self. I should've been there, but I gave up too easily. I let one asshole stand in my way and crush my dreams, and that regret haunted me every single day. I feared my friendship with Ru was over. Maybe I didn't deserve his love after all? I also feared my career in television was over. Maybe I wasn't good enough for it anyway? The world was passing me by. My life was passing me by. And before long, I fell into a constant state of anxiety: stressed, depressed, out of control, and full of fear.

Then, one day, I was drawing a bath for my then seven year-old daughter, Lola, and it hit me. It felt like someone had snuck up behind me with a Taser and held it to my head. Zzzzzzapppp! Zzzzzappp! Zzzzzappp! I felt a buzzing sensation that started at the back of my head and then suddenly, I couldn't breathe. My throat was closing. My heart was racing. I could barely speak or even swallow. Lillie, my then nine-year-old, ran into the bath-room when she heard the commotion. "9-1-1," I said. "Mommy!" she said. "What's wrong?" She started freaking the freak out, when she saw my ghastly pale face. "Call 9-1-1!" I said again, this time a little bit louder. *Heart attack*, I thought.

By the time the ambulance had arrived, so did my husband, who'd raced home from tae kwon do. (Lillie had called him to come home.) He was as white as the martial arts uniform he was wearing. I'll never forget the look of sheer horror on his face. The paramedics quickly gave me oxygen, strapped me to a gurney, and wheeled me out of the house as concerned neighbors looked on. I was certain that I was close to death and all I could think about was my girls. I couldn't die. Not yet. I needed to be there for my daughters.

And then, about halfway to the hospital, that crippling pain just—poof!— disappeared. Just like that. I was relieved mostly, though also a little embarrassed for scaring the hell out of everyone for what was apparently not my untimely death. Girl, I know how to make an exit, but that was even a bit much for me. I remember going from thinking about my daughters growing up without a mother to cracking jokes in the back of the ambulance. "Sorry my fat ass gave you boys a hernia when you lifted my gurney up into the ambulance. Put it on my tab." When I got to the hospital, I saw a cardiologist, who gave me a complete workup. "It's not your heart," he said. "It's your stress. You had an anxiety attack." In other words, it wasn't my heart. It was my *heart*.

If you've never experienced an anxiety attack, lucky you. They're horrible, awful things. Every physical sensation you feel in your body is 100 percent real—the pain, the racing heart, the labored breath. The cause, however, is unknown. In some people they are trigged by certain situations, such as large crowds or television cameras. Those aren't my triggers, thank God. You know I'm in my element when in front of a camera, surrounded by my girls and gays. No, what triggered mine was acute stress, this feeling that my life was spinning totally out of control, because I wasn't living it as I'd wanted to. My own life felt out of control. *I* felt out of control.

That day, as I was lying in my hospital bed, I decided to change my life on the spot. I was sick of sitting at home, doing nothing but eating out of boredom and depression, feeling sorry for myself. I was d-o-n-e, done. I had to be, if not for me, then for my kids. It was time to get my act together. And in the not-so-far back of my mind, I thought, *If Ru ever decides to give me another shot to be on his show, I need to be ready.* If I was going to be a diva again, I had to start first calming the f*ck down, and second, believing in myself again. And if I could do those two things, then maybe, just maybe, I'd be ready for bigger opportunities whenever they came to me.

So, that day, I went home and threw away my Cheetos. Step 1, accomplished. Step 2: I hired a trainer, even though I couldn't really afford one. (I actually worked out a deal with him that if he trained me for a cut rate and it worked, I'd tell everyone about it, proving once again when I put my mind to it, I can always make money with my mouth, especially when a sexy, sweaty man is involved.) I will shout out Marcus Nisbett and his Ncognito Fitness team in Wellington, Florida, for changing my life. Seriously. I looked better when I turned forty than I had when I was twenty. No lie. Step 3: I started to meditate, not well and not for long stretches of time, but for a few measly minutes every morning. And whenever I started getting down on myself, I looked that bitch in the mirror and said, "Oh no, you better don't." It's not as if a month later, I was a skinny zen master (it took me a full year of training six days a week/one hour a day to lose fifty-five pounds), but I summoned every drop of patience I had and waited (and waited and waited) until I could see the results. (I tell you this because we live in such a culture of instant gratification that some people think if they look at a dumbbell and don't get a bulging bicep immediately, they've failed. Not true. Don't give up on yourself.) And honestly, even if my plan was to make rainbow-colored spaghetti and wear a tutu, the fact that I had a plan at all gave me the thing I was missing most: a sense of control over my life.

It's easy to say, of course: Stay calm, believe in yourself, don't panic when success is happening for everyone around you except you. But thanks to having lived through both sides of this, I've learned a few trusty techniques for keeping your mental and emotional composure under extreme stress. Use my tricks whenever you're feeling overwhelmed, overlooked, or just plain lonely, and I swear to you, you'll feel instantly calmer, more centered, and ready for your big moment.

Find a therapist you love.
Seriously. It doesn't mean you're f*cked up. In fact, it means just the opposite, because thanks to therapy, you won't be. I started going at age sixteen, when my high school principal sent me

to one on threat of expulsion, claiming I had an unusual and insatiable need for attention. Now, I *hardly* think that's a problem. By the way, neither did my shrink. I loved going to therapy. I loved sorting through any shit that was on my mind, and while I'm seeing a different therapist now from the one I saw in high school, I still look forward to my regular talk sessions. Sometimes just putting words to whatever is bothering you is enough to make it stop bothering you. Something along those lines that is completely free is right at your fingertips: Google. When I would have anxiety attacks or symptoms, I would Google "anxiety symptoms" and just logging on to some of the websites that sell their programs (you don't have to buy them to look on the sites) and browsing through the list of physical symptoms helps me see that this happens to plenty of other people and for some reason that calms my mind to know that I am not alone in this hell. Now, if you can't afford therapy, or my Google trick doesn't help, try my backup: yoga. It quiets the mind in much the same way, and you get to not feel guilty for once about wearing yoga pants all day, too. PS: If you can't afford yoga class, there are some great DVDs out there that do the job just fine. Light a candle in your living room and down dog until the cows come home. Namaste, girl.

Be present.

A more highfalutin way to say that is "force consciousness." A more low-falutin' way to say that is "wake the f*ck up, diva." You can't go through your life in a haze, unless said haze is being produced by a strategically placed smoke machine at your feet.

We each have so much going on in our lives that it's easy to stop paying careful attention to what we're doing and just start going through the motions. That's how you lose your heart, and a diva without heart is as sad as a gay without glitter. When you find yourself going to a bad place, pull yourself out of the situation and ask yourself these three questions: What am I doing? Why am I doing this? And what is it going to get me? I sometimes even ask these questions of myself *out loud*, like a crazy person, but I don't care. It helps. And you know what else? You might as well come to terms with the fact that even if you're operating with a Buddha-level focus, you're still going to make shitty decisions sometimes. But if you make good ones, positive ones, *conscious* ones 80 percent of the time, then you win.

Get some perspective.

Ru and I talk about our place in the world a lot, and whenever we get on the subject of our egos and how they play into our happiness, you could basically time how long it takes before one of us starts quoting (or misquoting) Eckhart Tolle's *Power of Now*. If you've heard us gabbing about our life philosophies on our podcasts—yeah, we usually get real deep right before our conversations turn to lace-front wigs—then you know that we're sort of obsessed with the idea that the present is all you've ever got. When Ru can't ground himself and my quickly Googled quotes aren't helping him, he looks at Google Earth. Knowing he's just a tiny speck in this ginormous universe brings him comfort. Me? Google Earth makes me freak out! What? I'm just a tiny speck?

THE

TDIVAS HAVE THE POWER TO RISE ABOVE all the noise in life that drowns out everyone else's thoughts and desires, and eventually sinks them. We stay focused when others get frazzled, lively when others get lazy, hopeful when others start to hate, and determined when others get disillusioned. And though we're constantly and secretly working our amazingly tight little asses off to do just that, we make it look effortless to everyone else. Divas who keep the faith in themselves know that even if the phone is deafeningly silent right now, it could start ringing off the hook at any given moment. Yes, you're *that* great. And when other people actually take the time to notice that, then you've got to be in top form, mind and body, ready to be in the spotlight immediately. If you're not ready, you may miss your big moment, and there'll be no one to blame for it but yourself.

Don't worry about things you can't change, and don't complain about things you can. That's the diva code. Live by it, and you'll stay centered, so when it's time, you'll be able to take center stage. This quote shall now be your mantra: If you *stay* ready, you won't have to *get* ready. You're welcome.

Nothing matters? Nooooo! So, instead, when I need a reality check, I like to peek in on my daughters in their beds at night, after they fall asleep. The love I feel for them is what grounds me. It reminds me what really matters in this world. If you're not sure what grounds you, then start looking for a touchstone. Every diva needs one. It may not look blingy, but that doesn't mean it's not a gem.

Meditate.

I'm still a newbie at this, but I'm getting better and feeling better because of it too. The growing body of scientific research on the health benefits of meditation is amazing. Studies show that just sitting quietly for a few minutes a day may help with everything from lowering stress and anxiety to preventing cancer and heart disease. I recommend it, and I hope you're better at it than me. Basically here's how my quiet mind looks: *Ok, Michelle, clear your head. Ooooo but that nail art I just pinned on Pinterest . . . OMG! I got my blue tick on Twitter! Finally! Yummmm Zac Efron took a shirtless selfie, I am soooo glad he joined Instagram . . . OMMMMM . . .* If, like me, your mind goes toward all the things you have to do and shit you have to buy, grab a pen and paper and get it all out before you close your eyes. I am the queen of to-do lists, but I don't call them that. Too boring. Diva, we call them our ta-da! lists.

Give up the illusion of control.

I used to stress, like really almost break, over every world problem I could think of: war, terrorism, global warming, Ebola, *Drag*

Race going on without me. At some point, you've got to come to terms with the fact that you can't control every damn thing. Some things are just out of your hands, and you've got to make peace with that. I'm not going to personally make world peace happen. I can't personally control what ISIS does. I can't clean up after Fukishima with Dove soap and latex gloves. So, my only choice is to sit here and be a bundle of nerves, wracked with worry—or to make like "Adele Dazeem" and "Let It Go." I've chosen to let it go, and I've become much calmer since giving it all up to the heavens. (And by that, I don't mean in some Jesus-y sort of way, though if he's your savior, hallelujah for you. If *My Little Pony* is your savior, then I salute, too, your Rainbow Dash. Who or what you believe in [or don't for that matter] is your choice. Have at it.) I've said to the universe, "I'm giving every day to you. You're in control of the big stuff. I'm in control of everything else." And once I did that, I felt much less anxiety and a greater sense of calm.

Let go of little things.

Years and years ago, long before my anxiety issues, a friend of mine once told me, "You live with such strength and power that one day, you're going to f*cking break." He was right. When I got mad, I'd throw shit. When I'd get happy, I'd bounce across the room. And eventually I discovered that when I got super-stressed, I dropped to my knees in pain and made my daughter call 911. That day, I snapped. I really think it's a risk factor of being a diva. As you may know, we're prone to drama. And not just for laughs, but sometimes we really feel the joy, the sorrow, the pain, all of our emotions more deeply than other people. It can be a wonderful quality in happy times and a wretched one in trying times. But in that moment in the hospital bed, I decided to make it my new policy to take a breath and take a moment to turn down my temperature when I get frustrated or sad. There is no reason to throw a cell phone at a wall, or honk your horn in rage when some jerk cuts you off, or have a panic attack because you weren't available to join your best friend on his TV show for the first two seasons.

RULE _no._ 21:

IF YOU TAKE NO FOR AN ANSWER *TWICE*, YOU'RE F*CKING UP.

You may love your job. You may love the people you work with. You may even love your boss. But, no matter how chummy you all are, when it really comes down to it, no one in your office is ultimately going to look out for your career as well as you will. That shouldn't come as a shocker, either, especially if you think of your workplace like *Drag Race's* workroom. (Of course, your office probably doesn't smell like eau de sweaty hip pads, but still.) The contestants usually help each other in the workroom. They become friends. Some more experienced queens will even take on a mentor role to the younger ones. But at the end of the day, everyone knows that only one queen can win, and each will do whatever she can to make sure it's her. Everyone plays hard, but also fair.

And then every once in a while at work, like on *Drag Race*, a horrible person will enter the fold, someone who would, as Bianca del Rio once put it, "sneak in your room at night and cut up all your wigs." If it's a coworker or underling, you can probably shut her down on your own with a quick, honest confrontation. But if your boss is the one who is being purposefully nasty to you—he's claiming your successes as his own, he keeps you out of important meetings, he prevents you from realizing your true potential—then, baby, you're in a real tough spot. To not let him mess with your own success, you've got to be smarter. Do your job, kick ass at it, make a reputation for yourself as a hard worker, and make friends. You'll need their support. And if that doesn't do the trick and your boss blatantly tries to block your success *repeatedly*, there is no question in my mind: You've got to get the hell out of there. #ByeFelicia! You cannot win if the person standing in front of you is purposely blocking your light, hogging your applause, or hip-checking you off the stage before you have a chance to walk your walk.

That's exactly what happened to me in West Palm Beach. The station was called Sunny 104.3, but should've been called Shaaaaady 104.3. As I related a few chapters ago, when I asked my boss for permission to tape season one of *Drag Race*, he issued me an unconditional "no," claiming that by taking my seat next to Ru at the judges' table, I would harm the station's otherwise wholesome image. At first, I thought it was just a managerial mistake on his part, but eventually I came to realize that, due to his personal prejudices, working under him and fulfilling my destiny were mutually exclusive endeavors.

By the time Ru was prepping for season three of *Drag Race*, the hurt I'd caused him by abandoning him for season one had at last faded, and all was fine again. Ru is on the show, as he is in real life: sweet, spiritual, gentle, and caring. He naturally plays the mother figure to all these queens, but he knew that to grow *Drag Race*'s ratings, it needed more than a drag mother and her fashionista friends. It also needed a loving but loud-mouthed aunt, one whom you can count on to make slightly inappropriate but always spot-on comments. So when World of Wonder called me to ask me for the second time if I'd take my rightful seat next to my best friend at the judges' table, I wasn't going to let anyone stop me.

The next day, after I finished my morning show, I took off my pink, fuzzy headphones and marched down the hall and into my boss's office to ask him, once again, for his permission to tape *Drag Race*. Once again, I had it all planned out how I could tape the show without it affecting my radio job whatsoever, but we never even got that far. "Listen," I said. "I've been asked to be a judge on *Drag Race* again. The show's a huge hit, and . . ." He cut me off before I could even finish my sentence, and without ever looking up from his papers, he said, "No." Just like that. "No." I stood there stunned for a minute, and not knowing quite what else to do, I stormed out of his office, slamming the door behind me.

I was so upset that by the time I reached the parking lot I was practically hyperventilating. You know what I did next? I'm a little embarrassed to tell you, but f*ck it: I called my Kabbalah teacher. (I know, I know, it sounds so disgustingly pretentious, but you'll have to forgive me. I was on a Jewish mysticism kick at the time. Who wasn't?) Anyway, she said to me, while wind chimes—die casts of Ashton Kutcher's balls, no doubt—clinged and clanged in the background, "You are at a crossroads in your life. You can either stay and have your security, knowing that things will never change, or you can push yourself, make a change, and make a difference. This is your big moment. What are you going to do with it?"

It was good spiritual counsel, but when a diva is in distress, it's wise to get some practical girlfriend guidance too. I couldn't exactly turn to Ru in this moment, because I did NOT want him to know that the boss had said no again, so I called my other best friend, Leah Remini. When I told her what had happened, she was basically the opposite of a wind chime. She handed me my ass over the phone. "You just walked out? What the f*ck is wrong with you?" she said in her thick Brooklyn accent. "It's not every day that a TV show drops into your lap. I don't care what you have to do, but you have to take this job! I'm going to call Les. Do you want me to call Les?" The "Les" she was referring to was Les Moonves, the president of CBS. Sunny 104.3, my radio station, happened to be a CBS radio station. "Les is TV, not radio," I protested, weakly. "Then I will call the head of CBS radio," she said, to which I responded, "He won't even know who I am! I'm in Market forty-seven in West Palm Beach, not number one." I was selling myself short, and Leah knew it. "You're one of his stars. Of course he knows who you are," she said. "Give me his number. I'll call him." I wasn't having it. "What, are you my mother now?" I said. But Leah kept her cool. "Then be a big girl, and you f*cking call him now."

When I got home, thanks to Leah's, let's call it "encouragement,"

THE

MOST PEOPLE IN THE WORLD ARE GOOD.

I truly believe that with all my heart. But every once in a while you run into someone who isn't, and if that someone happens to be your boss, then you've got to figure out how to deal with it. If he purposefully prevents you from succeeding once, cut him some slack. Maybe he made a mistake. Maybe you caught him on an insecure day. Maybe he doesn't know what he's doing, and he'll learn. So, if that's the case, keep your head down, do what you do best, and win him over or work around him. But if he shuts you down twice, then understand that, like on *Drag Race,* in order for you to win, only one of you can stay. The other must sashay away. Had I just listened to my boss and turned Ru down for the second time, I would've lost not only an amazing career opportunity, but also the most important friendship of my life. Being a strong, successful diva and being a good friend are two of my most essential core values. They're what make me who I am, so why on earth would I let some random's negativity stop me? I let it happen once. I'll never let it happen again. Divas, you know who you are. You've got a destiny to fulfill. Don't let anyone stand in your way.

I decided to call Scott Herman, executive vice president of CBS Radio. Now, this may come as a shocker to you, but people in positions of power have *always* intimidated me, and though we were acquainted, I was so nervous about talking to him that even my vagina was sweating. But I gathered my courage, I pointed my Vornado on that bitch, and I dialed the phone. When he picked up, he seemed actually thrilled to hear from me. And, the upside with Scott is this: I LOVED him. Yes, he was corporate, but he was (and still is) one of the real radio dudes left in the business. Incidentally, Scott used to listen to me when I did morning in NYC, so he knew with whom he was dealing. I told him my situation: I'd like to take five weeks of unpaid vacation to tape *RuPaul's Drag Race*, but my manager thought my participation in the show would reflect negatively on the station. Scott listened patiently and when I finished talking, he just said, "I have absolutely no problem with you doing that. I think it sounds great! Have fun!" I was so relieved to have his blessing. And you know what? A week later, Dockers was gone. Fired. To this day, I'm not sure if his rapid departure had anything to do with me, or if he was failing in other ways, too, but for whatever reason, I know he got what he deserved. And when I arrived in LA to shoot the show, I sat my happy ass next to Ru at that judges' table, he smiled, gave me a huge hug, and just said, "Now the show can begin." That was all I needed to hear. The bitch was back.

RULE <u>no.</u> 22:

STOP RELYING ON THAT BODY.

Take a little sashay down memory lane with me for a moment, will you? It's season three of *Drag Race*. I'm sitting at the judges' table next to Ru, watching all the beautiful queens walk the runway: Raja, Manila Luzon, Shangela, Yara Sofia, and out comes the immaculately gorgeous Carmen Carrera, showing off, well, what she'd always showed off: her mile-long legs, sexy waist, and invisible tuck. Early on, she was one of my absolute favorites. I mean, I could not stop looking at her. She was just so damn stunning, she practically made me pop a lady boner. But by the fourth episode, when she walked out once again in her barely there ensemble, I went in my head, *Oh, okaaaay. You're naked— again. Great. Snooze.* I was not impressed. We'd basically seen her skin every episode and "oooed and ahhed" over it and by this one, frankly, I was getting bored with the same old schtick. I wondered what else, if anything, she had to offer. So, in five little words that will forever be immortalized in the single "Runway Girl" by Ru and DJ Shyboy (ahem, available on iTunes, baby), I let her know that I'd had enough of what she was serving. With nothing but love in my heart, I warned her, "Stop relying on that body," and to my surprise (and don't you know, delight), it became *the* catchphrase of the season.

Honestly, I would've been more impressed by Carmen if she'd walked out wearing a circus lion-tamer's outfit, something to prove she was more than a one-trick ponytail. But episode after episode, it became clear that she believed—and I'd vehemently argue, mistakenly so—that her body was not just her biggest asset, but also her *only* asset. And hear me out here, divas: No matter how flawless you are when you wake up, the very moment you start believing your body is the only thing you've got to offer, you not only become predictable (and therefore—gasp!—boring), but you also run the danger of becoming unhealthy.

Before I go on with that thought, I first want to make clear that I love Carmen. Since she appeared on the show, she's grown immensely as a performer, and a person, and it's because she's finally realized she's so much more than just a hot body. I hope I had something to do with her having that epiphany, but even if I didn't, I'm really proud of her evolution.

Anyway, I'm very, very passionate about this rule, because it's one I had to learn the very hard way. When I was a just baby Visage—picture little ol' me in high school—I heard some boys making fun of my mom for being fat, and I suppose that that's when I first got it into my head that skinny must be better and more desirable, and being desired means being noticed. As I started getting more and more self-conscious about my body, I started to eat less and less. My parents were strict meat-and-potatoes, and bread-and-butter, people, and soon enough, every night at dinner, I'd chew my food, stuff it into my cheeks, excuse myself from the table ("I have to go to the bathroom"), and flush it down the toilet. Dinnertime suddenly involved about two faithful trips to the loo, and surprisingly, my parents never even took note or if they did, maybe they just thought I was being a moody teenager. By my senior year, the purging had started. I couldn't handle puking—bulimia in the traditional way wasn't for me—so I chose to eliminate the little food I'd eaten the only other way I knew how. I mistakenly thought that by taking laxatives every day the calories that I put in my mouth would be flushed out of my body before they could be absorbed (and turned into fat).

My disordered eating continued—and even worsened—all throughout my early twenties. My laxative habit was easy to hide, when I was home in New York, Vogueing in the clubs, and competing in the body category in the Harlem balls, but when I was on the road with Seduction, it got to be a little more challenging. Not to be crude, but you can only slam laxatives when you know you're going to be near a bathroom in a few hours. Desperate to remain thin (and, thus, the center of attention, I thought), I was constantly scouting toilets, and as a result, my life started to feel—in more ways than one—completely shitty.

When I did eat, my meals were in no way healthy or complete. I subsisted mainly just on coffee and cigarettes. Eventually, Sinoa caught onto me. She said, "Michelle, put your hands on your hips." I struck a hammy pose, and she held her hands up in front of her face to mime framing a camera shot of me. "Yep," she said. "You look just like Mr. Salty." Now, if you're too young to know who Mr. Salty is, screw you. Just kidding, I'm just jealous. Mr. Salty was the sailor-hat-wearing mascot to Nabisco's pretzel sticks. His arms and legs were made of pretzel sticks, giving him a very lanky look. She went on, "Seriously, I'm really worried about you. You've gotten so skinny." At 5'4", I was not much more than ninety pounds. Whenever she started to get on my case—by the way, thank you for that, Sinoa!—I'd join her for breakfast, when I'd have a few cups of coffee and maybe a strip of bacon or a bite of an omelet.

I wasn't consciously starving myself. If you'd asked me then if I was, I would've looked at you like you were from Mars. But the truth was, I was completely and wholly and unhealthily relying on my body. I would walk around naked—or as close to naked as I could get away with—at every chance I got. Even when I went to the Jersey shore, which was full of leering meatheads, I'd wear nothing but a G-string. My ridiculous ass and surgically enhanced, albeit still smallish tits, I thought, were the best things I had to offer the world, and I'd use them to get the attention I so desperately craved. Which is ironic, because I wouldn't do it at a strip club. I couldn't get paid for it—it had to be on MY dime, not anyone else's. Plus, I figured, attention is attention. Even if you look at me and think I'm too skinny, if you look at me and worry, if you look at me and think *anything* at all, you're still looking at me, and that's the point. I didn't care whether you were ogling or concerned. To me, all of it felt like fawning, and I ate it up. It fulfilled me in a way I thought food never could.

THE T

IF YOU HAVE A BIG, JUICY ASS OR NICE TITS, then by all means, flaunt what you've got. Werk it, girl! Feel fierce. I fully support nudity, especially when you've got a body like Carmen Carrera's or Madonna's. But know this: Your body is not who you are, and it's not *all* that you have to offer to the world. And if you rely solely on your T&A for your self-worth, you will never be happy. Never. Because by doing so, you're handing your power over to other people. Strangers, even. If you can grab their attention, you'll feel good about yourself. And if you can't, you'll feel destroyed, wanting, worthless. Divas, I beg of you: Hold on to your power. Rely on your talents, your wits, your voice, your creativity, and your heart, and if you can do that, I guarantee you, you will always get noticed, and you will always feel beautiful.

Then, when I was twenty-six, I got a wake-up call. My boyfriend, Michael, the man I thought I was going to marry, broke up with me out of the blue over the phone after four years of dating. Feeling heart-shattered and lost, I walked into my bathroom, reached for my laxatives, and swallowed every pill in the box. I can't remember how many pills were in the box, but I think it was about twenty-four. I wasn't trying to kill myself or anything. (That would've been an incredibly shitty way to go. Badump bump.) But I was grasping for any sense of control I could get. If I couldn't control my relationships, I could at least control my body, and again, that's all I thought I had to offer. *These will flatten my stomach,* I thought. *If I'm going to be single again, I've got to look my best—and fast.*

I ended up writhing alone and in pain on my bathroom floor, so cramped I thought I was literally going to poop my intestines out. I probably should've gone to the hospital that day, but I never did, and the next day, when the agony finally subsided, I swore off laxatives forever and changed my goal. I vowed to get strong and healthy, whatever that meant for me, not just thin. I literally joined a gym that next day, ate three square meals a day, and started to look at myself in an entirely new way. I had so much more to offer the world than my tits and ass. I had my talent and let's not forget . . . my voice.

I learned a lesson that so many of my girls and gays struggle with their whole lives. I was relying on my body for my happiness, and that is a huge fallacy. Your body is not your happiness. Even if you lose those last five, or ten, or fifty pounds, all the things in your life that suck will still suck after you do. Plus, you'll be hungry. And no matter how much attention you get for being sexy, take it from me, it'll *never* be enough to make you feel whole. I mean, I gyrated on stage nearly naked in front of arenas of 60,000 screaming fans, and it still wasn't enough to make me feel happy. That's the damn truth. Besides, let's face it: Eventually your tits are going to sag and your balls are going to drag, and if they're your only source of joy, you're going to have a hell of a hard road ahead.

Now, I listen to my body. I pay attention to it. I nurture it. I eat consciously, enriching it with every bite, rather than starving it, or poisoning it with processed, preservative-filled foods. I go to the gym, I hike, and I loves me a good spin class. I treat myself with kindness and respect. And as a result, I feel not only a million times healthier and more energized, but also so much more comfortable and confident in my skin. I used to say beauty is on the inside, but I just said it because I knew that's what I was supposed to feel. Honestly, it was just lip service. But the older I get, the more I really do honestly and truly believe it. Some of the ugliest people I've ever met have been drop-dead gorgeous on the outside, and some of the most beautiful people I know wouldn't necessarily stand out in a crowd at first glance. And no matter what size I am, I now know in my heart of hearts that I *am* beautiful. And guess what? I know you are, too.

RULE _no._ 23:

MAKE MAGIC.

Ladies, get yourself a magic wand—and use it. And by that, I mean a Hitachi Magic Wand.

Stress is a bitch, and in a book of my best life advice for my divas, I'd be remiss if I didn't include this little mind-calming, muscle-relaxing nugget for all my girls: The next time you're about to spend sixty dollars on a cheap pair of shoes or an utterly forgettable dinner, do yourself a favor and don't. Instead, save up that cash and go get yourself this Japanese-made back massager (wink, wink), available everywhere from your local drugstore to your local sex shop. Take it home, use it on your back, and then a little lower, lower, lowwwer, lowwwwer—for CHRISSAKES, LOWER!—there! Catch my drift? Boys, you're out on this one, unless you truly do have aching muscles (not the love muscle), then this is a beauty you could enjoy as well.

YOU DESERVE TO FEEL GOOD. And you don't have to rely on anyone else to make that happen. You are magic, honey. Love yourself. Only, I recommend loving yourself on the low setting.

RULE _no._ 24:

MAKE YOUR BOSS LOOK GOOD.

No matter how talented, unique, charismatic, or nervy you are, it is impossible to make it to the top alone. Nobody succeeds alone. You need fans—lots of them—in high places, low places, and those hard-to-reach places. In fact, to realize your full diva potential, you need to be so beloved that all the people around you— from your boss to your buddies, from the fella pumping your gas to the fella pumping your . . . well, you know—feel an almost inexplicably overwhelming desire to please you, help you, elevate you, and make you happy.

So, how do you do that? Well, first, ever so subtly, figure out who holds the power. When you're at work, whether you clock in at a factory, office, school, or Radio City Music Hall, that's easy. The one person in particular who can help (or hinder) you more than anyone else is your boss. Do not shy away. You're not going to get noticed by keeping your head buried in your cubicle.

Once you've got the boss's attention, there are pretty much two schools of thought when it comes to handling such a top: The first believes you should go full on Eve Harrington on her Bette Davis ass. That is, think of the job she's doing now as one that rightfully belongs to you. Study her, insinuate yourself into her inner circle, and exploit her flaws, and eventually you'll be able to take her down so you can take her place. There are pros and cons to using this sort of get-ahead tactic. The pro: It can be quite effective, if you're willing to go all in. The con: Your horrid soul may just rot from the inside out. The *All About Eve* approach is just such a negative, lonely, and cynical way to succeed. You'll never win fans by tearing other people down, and even if you do, they won't be the kind who'll stick by your side for very long.

I have a smarter alternative for my divas: Do exactly the opposite. Rather than search for your boss's flaws, amplify her strengths, compensate for her weaknesses, and make her shine more than a cheap starlet's forehead under heavy lights. Basically, just do whatever you need to do to make her look like she's got a glowing halo hovering over her angelic head. After all, she's got people to impress too—execs, clients, customers—and she'll be grateful for your help. Soon, she'll learn to trust you and rely on you, and you will become indispensable to her. And the more she appreciates you, the more eager she'll be to give you new opportunities, promotions, and raises. Cha-ching! Everybody wins.

This has been my business philosophy for dealing with authority figures from pretty much high school on, but by the time I was Vogueing in the clubs, a couple of genius guys made it official. They wrote some supposedly groundbreaking article in the *Harvard Business Review* about the merits of "managing up," in which, as I understand it, they explained for the first time ever the benefits of making the people above you look and feel good. Lord knows I didn't read the article at the time. Girl, I was too busy living it. It's always been the cornerstone of my success.

One of the clearest, crassest, and most transactional examples of how well this philosophy works is in a strip club. (Who knows? Maybe that's even where those Harvard scholars got the idea in the first place.) I put it to work every night back in my days of emceeing the hot-oil wrestling at Goldfingers in Queens. Step 1: Find who has the power. I started each shift by hanging back and scanning the room, looking for the audience member who had the most sway (e.g., money) to make my night a success. Once I spotted the biggest spender—usually the guy out with his buddies for a bachelor party—I'd play to him as if he were my boss. In a sense, he was, since he was the one paying my bills (with his bills). Step 2: Find out what he needs to feel good. I'd chat him up, trying to get a sense of what kind of night he was looking for. Did he want to feel big or small? In or out of control? Dirty or clean? Step 3: Make up for his weaknesses by playing to his strengths. With the mic in my hand, I controlled the pacing of the night. If he seemed embarrassingly eager, I'd use my wit and my sense of humor—two of my assets—to slow things down, so he wouldn't look like an ass in front of his friends or the wrestlers. If he was too timid to get in the ring, I'd build him up until he felt like every woman's greatest dream. When he had a good night, *I* had a better night.

THE

IF YOU WANT TO GET AHEAD, YOU'VE GOT TO DO MORE THAN JUST YOUR JOB. Showing up on time, doing your work well, being your gorgeous self: All those things will earn you job security, and if you stay put for long enough, eventually you'll move up the ladder. But real divas don't like to wait for what's handed to us. We demand it. We don't walk, we sashay. We don't glow, we radiate. We don't have style, we *make* style. And when it comes to earning accolades, whether in our theaters, clubs, or cubicles, we do whatever it takes to bring them on. The easiest way to earn praise is to make the people in power know, love, and trust us. When you turn on that charm, baby, everybody wins, but especially you.

Sometimes, I'll admit, it can be difficult to make your boss shine when your boss is an asshole, and all you want is for him to fail and disappear from your life forever. Girl, I've been there. And here's what you do: Suck it up. Men, especially, like their egos stroked (as well as other things, but stay away from that). Summon all your strength and slip in a compliment whenever you can. Be as flattering as you can without turning into a kiss ass. You'll know you've crossed that line when you start to feel dirty. If that happens, reel it in, or you'll lose your credibility and possibly also your work friends. I used to do this all the time in radio. If anybody was interviewing me, I'd say things like, "It's all thanks to our legendary program director," or "That's a question for my genius cohost here." The effort I had to exert to do that was minimal, and the payoff was great. And you know what? It might just be what your boss needs to open up to you. Look at Gail, the meanie I worked with at Casablanca and Fundamental Thiiiiiiings. She started out as an ice queen, and by the time I was done with her, she gave me wide latitude to pursue my music career even though I was on her clock. I even thanked her for it in the Seduction album notes.

Now, with Ru, it's a little different, because not only is he my boss on *Drag Race* (and before that on VH1's *The RuPaul Show*), but he's also my best friend. My love for him just makes me a bazillion times more invested in making him shine. Over our many years together, I've gotten to know him better than almost anyone else on the planet. It's like we can read each other's minds. One look, one curl of his lip, one bat of his gorgeous lashes, and I know exactly what he's thinking. So if we're doing an interview or a podcast or laying it out for the queens on *Drag Race*, I listen closely to him. I watch him. I've always got his back so he'll never stumble or be at a loss for words, and he knows it.

One day back in 1997, when we were sitting together in the backseat of a town car in the Holland Tunnel en route from our radio show, which we broadcast out of Jersey City, to *The RuPaul Show's* VH1 set in Midtown Manhattan, I turned to him and said, "I don't know if I'll ever have the words to thank you for what you've done for me, bringing me to VH1 with you and making yet another one of my dreams become a reality." He turned toward me, looked me dead in the eye, and said, "Bitch, I bring you along because you make me look good." And that was it, and it's true. I know my role. Ru knows that no matter what he says, I will pick him up. I will never let him fall. I will never let him feel awkward. And, in return, he'll guard me like a mother lion.

RULE no. 25:

BUILD YOUR LEGACY.

When you wake up every morning, before you even get out of bed, set your intention for the day. (Oh, shut up, you bitches. I know it sounds a little hokey, but just try it.) You don't have to say it out loud, but think of something you want to work on for the day. If you're feeling a little too controlling, it can be as simple as "I give this day to the universe." If you're feeling lost, try "Live what you love." If you're feeling unrelentingly bitchy, use "Be kinder than you feel." Or, for any given day, this diva mantra always works: "Keep calm and sparkle on." Your intention determines the way you are in the world, and the way you are builds your reputation. That rep will precede you wherever you go, so it's important not to f*ck it up. And you won't, if you follow every single rule I've given you. Heed my advice, and you'll become the diva you are, the rest of the world will know it, and you'll be golden.

Your reputation is everything. Well, *almost* everything. There's your legacy, too, which accounts for the rest of what matters in this life. If anything is worth doing, it's going to be part of your legacy. And if you're not sure if you're making the right decision, ask yourself, "After the lashes come off and the house lights come up, is this how I want to be remembered?" (If the answer is no, save your energy for something else.)

It is up to each of us to affect positive change in our lives. We can't just sit around complaining that things aren't fair without trying our damnedest to fix what's wrong. I'm not saying you need hunt down injustice, adopt "a cause," or join a march. (Which I am all for, but TBH, Divas are much better suited for riding on floats in parades anyway, thank you very much.) What I am saying, though, is that you need to find something that ignites passion within you and that your future self, or your future kids, or somebody else's future kids, will thank you for.

For me, I've always been a friend of the gays, but my passion is bigger than friendship. I want to make the world better for them and their families, because I want to make the world better for me and my family, *for all of us,* and that's one of the many reasons it was my dream to join Ru on *Drag Race.* I knew from the beginning that this show could change people's minds not only about the gay community, but also about the drag and transgender communities. In part because they are the most fabulous, they are also among the most feared, ridiculed, ostracized subsets of our society. And I believed the show would open up people's eyes to the fact that these kids are not only talented beyond belief, but also human. They're artists. They have feelings, raw talent, and more nerve than anyone else I know. Unlike Milton Berle in a dress, they're no joke. Drag is their livelihood, in that it's what makes them feel alive, and that's why I knew my soul needed to be a part of *Drag Race.* Not only are we changing people's minds about drag, but we're also bringing families together. Thanks to *Drag Race*, several queens, including Detox and Alyssa Edwards, have been reunited with their parents, and as a mother, that is a big f*ckin deal to me.

When kids come out of the closet, eventually they find other gays and build their community, but parents of gay children don't have that same automatic support network. Sure, there's PFLAG, an amazing organization (pflag.org), but some moms and dads can't even find the strength to reach out to it. Every day, I aspire to inspire *those* parents, to let them know they're not alone, and to remind them their *only* job is to love their kids unconditionally. And when I see them do that, it makes me so damn happy. Occasionally, a mother or father will come to one of my gigs or signings with their gay son or daughter. That's when the tears come to my eyes. I always take extra time to reach out to them and say thank you. Thank you for standing by your amazing child. If, through the show, touring, tweeting, talking on the radio, or just being my diva self, I can reach out and touch someone else, parent or child, to let them know they're not alone, then that will be part of my legacy.

And so will all the past contestants on *Drag Race*. In the past few years, I've gotten to know many of them very well. We travel the entire country (and often other countries) together for the *Battle of the Seasons* tour, and I've become the Fairy Dragmother to these children. I ride with them on the bus. I sleep next to them in sometimes nice, sometimes shitty, hotels. I have the privilege of watching them onstage night after night, and I've always been

THE TCHILDREN, IT'S NOT ABOUT FINDING THE RIGHT HEMLINE; IT'S ABOUT FINDING YOUR HAPPINESS. It's not about your swag; it's about your soul. It's not about lip-syncing; it's about love. It's always about love. So many times in life as we age, we tend to put our careers first, our kids first, our significant others first, and forget about us. It's time to reclaim your life and nurture that inner diva that lives within us all whether you are male, female, questioning or transitioning, we've all got an inner diva. You build your legacy every day by being who you are, so do what you love, take care of those you love, and always stay true to your heart. Now, go out there and werk!

amazed by them. When I see them become stronger performers—
and people—as a direct result of being on the show, I feel so
personally proud of each and every one of them.

So many queens come to *Drag Race*, shaking in their leopard-
print thongs at the sight of me, as if I was going to be mean to
them for the sheer sport of it. But if you get me at all and understand what I'm doing, then you'd know I'd never. Every single
word that comes out of my mouth on the show, and in life, is only
to help make these kids realize, and live up to, their own potential.

Sometimes, it's not always easy. In 2013, I was starring in
The Rocky Horror Show in San Antonio, Texas, for six weeks
with season six finalist Alaska Thunderf*ck. (I was Magenta, of
course. He was Dr. Frank-N-Furter.) I hadn't known Alaska very
well prior to the show, but we rented a house together for the
duration. Every night onstage, I got to watch his genius—and
that's really what it was. Pure genius. He had more star power
and talent that anyone gave him credit for. (At the time, he was
dating my good friend and season four winner, Sharon Needles,
who always took top billing. When Sharon was in the room,
there just wasn't enough oxygen left for Alaska's star to shine,
even though, if given the chance, Alaska could be at times even
more brilliant.) After we came off the stage and drove back home
together every night—no makeup, no pretense—I'd watch him
struggle with finding his place in the world. He was miserable,
and the only thing that made him less so was a half-empty bottle
of Maker's Mark. Eventually, I had to say something. I told him,
"Alaska, I don't understand why you're doing this to yourself,

because you're so talented." We talked all night, we cried a lot, and by the end of our show's run, he kicked the booze altogether. My sweet Lasky has been sober for more than a year, and shining brighter than he ever has before because he is allowing his brilliance to beam through. I am so. Damn. Proud.

Ru always says everybody has to have their own process, and other people shouldn't hinder that process. Everybody just has to go through all they have to go through, until they decide they've had enough. Me? I believe it helps to have a facilitator, and for all of my drag children, that's exactly what I consider myself. When I see that you're stuck in any given place in your life, I'll not only help open a new door for you, but I'll also walk through it with you. I do not, however, sugarcoat anything, and I give it to 'em raw, because that's how most of them like it. Ahem. Anyone who has ever taken a journey with me—and that, by the way, includes you, too, now—is a part of my legacy. If I can make life better for one diva, then I'll be living. And *living*.

ACKNOWLEDGMENTS

I'd like to acknowledge the many great people who have helped me make this book dream become a reality: First and foremost my husband, David, because without him none of this life I am living could exist. Thank you for always pushing me beyond anything I would normally do because I can be lazy at times (yes, I said it!). I love you. My daughters Lillie, and Lola, for always being my shining beacons of light and making me want to be a stronger, kinder, better woman. There is no greater love than the love I have for you. You make me want to laugh louder, fight harder, dig deeper, and be the best friend, mother, and woman that I can possibly be. Thank you for never allowing me to settle for mediocrity. You girls are my constant inspiration. My dad, Marty, and my mother, Arlene, without whom none of this would be. Thank you for running me to every audition, coming to every play, sitting through every concert, and always, irrevocably standing by my side, though Mommy is doing it from heaven. Aunt Harriet for being a surrogate mom to me and grandmother to my girls. I am grateful that through you, a piece of their grandma lives on. My literary agent, Holly Bemiss, and her amazing wife, Erin Bried, for believing in me and, quite literally, always having my back, getting my vision and hearing my true voice. What a great ride this has been! Emily Haynes, my incredible editor at Chronicle Books, for giving me such a wide berth to create this diva masterpiece and not trying to fit me into a mold that already existed. Michael Morris, my book designer, who, I think, shares my eyes, as he created magic and all I could do was drool over the final product. My entire Chronicle Books family for not even thinking twice about taking this journey with me, thank you so very much. Randy Barbato, Fenton Bailey, Thairin Smothers, and my entire World of Wonder family for always seeing the stardom in me even when I doubted it. You have the biggest balls of anyone I know and I am proud to call you my family. Lindsey Olliver for never, ever thinking twice about being there for me 100 percent of the time. I can always count on you. Laura Mazro for being the best friend a diva could ask for, through thick and thin you have always been my rock. Leah Remini, the world knows how talented and funny you are, but I know how caring and loving you are. THANK YOU for always being there for me, especially in times of need. To the entire LGBTQ community, who give me life all day, every day. My freaks, weirdos and misfits, I fight for you, for what you have given to me. Your love and loyalty make me feel like I can move mountains, and for that I will always be committed to you. RuPaul Andre Charles, I will never have the words to tell you how much you mean to me. You are a constant source of love and inspiration for me that I will never grow tired of. You are my sister, my brother, my best friend, and soul mate. You ARE every color in the crayon box. I love you to the moon and back for now and forever. THANK YOU, Ru, thank you.

PHOTO CREDITS

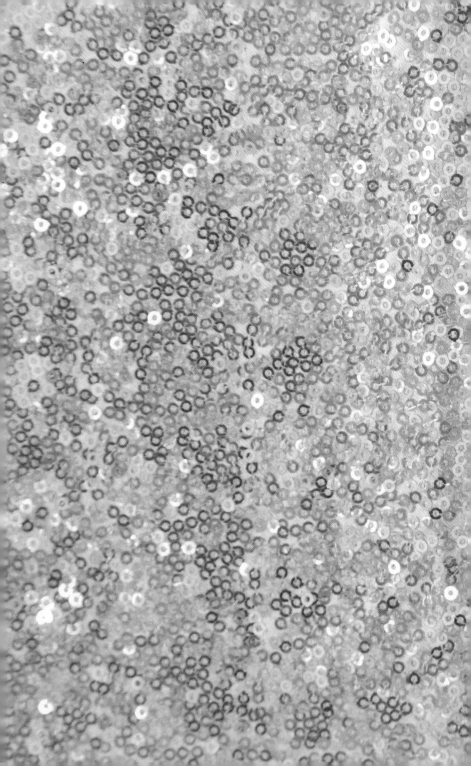

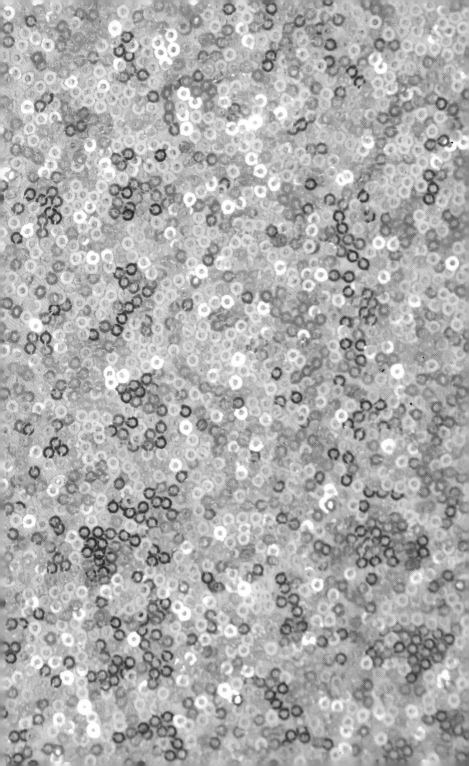